The Life of P. T. Barnum

Written by Himself

WITH RELATED DOCUMENTS

Edited with an Introduction by

Stephen Mihm

University of Georgia

bedford/st.martin's
Macmillan Learning
Boston | New York

For Bedford/St. Martin's

Vice President, Editorial, Macmillan Learning Humanities: Edwin Hill
Program Director for History: Michael Rosenberg
Senior Program Manager for History: William J. Lombardo
History Marketing Manager: Melissa Rodriguez
Director of Content Development: Jane Knetzger
Associate Editor: Mary Posman Starowicz
Assistant Editor: Alexandra DeConti
Content Project Manager: Lidia MacDonald-Carr
Senior Workflow Project Manager: Jennifer Wetzel
Production Assistant: Brianna Lester
Senior Media Project Manager: Michelle Camisa
Manager of Publishing Services: Andrea Cava
Project Management: Lumina Datamatics, Inc.
Composition: Lumina Datamatics, Inc.
Photo Researcher: Lenny Behnke
Permissions Manager: Kalina Ingham
Senior Art Director: Anna Palchik
Cover Design: William Boardman
Cover Photo: Library of Congress, Prints & Photographs Division, Reproduction number
LC-DIGppmsca-35586 (digital file from original item, front) LC-DIGppmsca-35587
(digital file from original item, back)
Printing and Binding: LSC Communications

Manufactured in the United States of America.

2 1 0 9 8 7
f e d c b a

For information, write: Bedford/St. Martin's, 75 Arlington Street, Boston, MA 02116

ISBN 978-1-4576-9206-2

Acknowledgments

Acknowledgments and copyrights appear on the same page as the text and art selections they cover; these acknowledgments and copyrights constitute an extension of the copyright page.

At the time of publication all Internet URLs published in this text were found to accurately link to their intended website. If you do find a broken link, please forward the information to history@macmillan.com so that it can be corrected for the next printing.

Foreword

The Bedford Series in History and Culture is designed so that readers can study the past as historians do.

The historian's first task is finding the evidence. Documents, letters, memoirs, interviews, pictures, movies, novels, or poems can provide facts and clues. Then the historian questions and compares the sources. There is more to do than in a courtroom, for hearsay evidence is welcome, and the historian is usually looking for answers beyond act and motive. Different views of an event may be as important as a single verdict. How a story is told may yield as much information as what it says.

Along the way the historian seeks help from other historians and perhaps from specialists in other disciplines. Finally, it is time to write, to decide on an interpretation and how to arrange the evidence for readers.

Each book in this series contains an important historical document or group of documents, each document a witness from the past and open to interpretation in different ways. The documents are combined with some element of historical narrative—an introduction or a biographical essay, for example—that provides students with an analysis of the primary source material and important background information about the world in which it was produced.

Each book in the series focuses on a specific topic within a specific historical period. Each provides a basis for lively thought and discussion about several aspects of the topic and the historian's role. Each is short enough (and inexpensive enough) to be a reasonable one-week assignment in a college course. Whether as classroom or personal reading, each book in the series provides firsthand experience of the challenge—and fun—of discovering, recreating, and interpreting the past.

Lynn Hunt
David W. Blight
Bonnie G. Smith

Preface

Once a household name throughout the English-speaking world, Phineas Taylor Barnum—better known as P. T. Barnum—has faded into obscurity. At best, his name lingers on today in the name of a circus he helped found later in life. As a consequence, it often surprises students to learn that Barnum's *Autobiography*, first published in 1855 and then revised and republished multiple times throughout the showman's life, became the bestselling autobiography of the nineteenth century and one of the bestselling books of all time. Its appeal is understandable. Unlike other popular tales of self-made men of the era—Benjamin Franklin's *Autobiography* being the most obvious—Barnum's life story offers a much lighter, picaresque tale of his rise to riches as a showman, impresario, huckster, and entertainer. It is not a story that suffers from seriousness.

While Barnum's autobiography is certainly entertaining, his colorful anecdotes and endless tales of practical jokes and impostures can mislead modern readers into viewing him as nothing more than a strange trickster who preyed on a vulnerable public. While unquestionably interesting, was he historically significant?

But this reading misses Barnum's enduring legacy. His ghost looms large over twenty-first-century business and culture. The modern entertainment industry—never mind the culture of celebrity with which it is intertwined—owes a profound debt to Barnum's innovations a century and a half ago. He understood, far better than his contemporaries, how to attract an audience, and no less important, how to keep it. In fact, the professions of advertising, public relations, marketing, and all the other means and methods used to persuade twenty-first-century consumers what to buy, where to eat, what to watch, and how to live arguably trace their origins to Barnum. In other words, while Barnum's tales of mock mermaids and celebrity opera singers can appear, at first glance, to belong to an era very different from our own, we in fact live in a world that Barnum helped create. He is with us still.

No less important is Barnum's legacy for capitalism. If Benjamin Franklin was the embodiment of what sociologist Max Weber termed the "Protestant ethic," P. T. Barnum was something else altogether. In his reckless speculations and shameless self-promotions, Barnum modeled another route to riches. His was a no-holds-barred brand of capitalism that continues to inspire—and horrify—to this day.

Part one helps situate Barnum's life in the larger economic transformations of the era as well as the nature of the mass entertainments that he helped pioneer. It also explores the origins and outsized influence of his autobiography, which quickly became the object of endless criticism, scrutiny, and even parody. Finally, the introduction situates Barnum's contributions within the larger issues of his lifetime, including the vexed issues of race, slavery, and abolition.

The particular version of his memoirs reproduced here is drawn from the original 1855 edition. Unlike subsequent versions, where Barnum banished some of the more disquieting stories and events of his life, the original edition offers the most unvarnished account of Barnum's career up until that time. It does, however, suffer from repetitions and digressions that often have little to do with Barnum's own life. These have been edited out in the interest of brevity, leaving behind a far more streamlined text for modern-day readers.

In addition to Barnum's life story, this edition reprints fourteen additional documents to bring Barnum's entire career to life. These documents include reviews of the autobiography in the popular press, selections from Barnum's other writings, and several other items selected to illuminate parts of his life not captured by the autobiography itself. The documents also include a handful of arresting visuals to illustrate how Barnum harnessed the power of images and advertising to advance his ends.

Following the documents there is a chronology, questions for consideration, and a selected bibliography to encourage further analysis and research.

ACKNOWLEDGMENTS

I have been fortunate to work with such a talented editorial team at Bedford/St. Martin's, including Program Director Michael Rosenberg, History Marketing Manager Melissa Rodriguez, Content Project Manager Lidia MacDonald-Carr, and Cover Designer William Boardman.

A special thanks to Associate Editor Mary Posman Starowicz, Assistant Editor Lexi DeConti and Senior Program Manager William Lombardo who have been unremitting in their attention and encouragement. I very much appreciate their advice and editorial acumen. Likewise, I owe a great debt of gratitude to the seven outside reviewers who took time out of their busy schedules to review the manuscript and offer constructive criticism.

In closing, I wish to thank my wife for her patience and understanding as this project has moved from the faintest glimmer of an idea to something real and substantial. During that time, our boys have grown from infancy to a veritable three-ring circus. Like the subject of this book, they are hilarious, endlessly entertaining, and a constant reminder not to take life too seriously.

Stephen Mihm

Contents

APPENDIXES

Illustrations

PART ONE

Introduction:
P. T. Barnum and the Business of Entertainment

The publication of Phineas Taylor Barnum's autobiography in December 1854 was, like everything else connected to the famed showman, an event fueled by publicity, controversy, and more than a little bit of money.

Barnum's book, which he sold to a New York City publisher for what was then the astronomical sum of $70,000 plus a generous cut of all future royalties, baffled some reviewers and unnerved others. "In this country, more perhaps than in any other," wrote the *New York Daily Times*, "[s]uccess is regarded as the test of worth . . . and Barnum is the embodiment and impersonation of success. From being poor and obscure, he has rapidly made himself very rich and very famous. As a natural consequence he is watched, admired and envied by hundreds of thousands who are as poor as he was, and who are anxious to be as rich as he is."

But for this reviewer, and for many others, the message of Barnum's book was dangerous. "What is the lesson it is likely to teach?" asked the *Times*, answering, "that his success has been achieved—his wealth acquired—his reputation and consideration established, by the systematic, adroit and persevering plan of *obtaining money under false pretenses from the public at large*." Little wonder this newspaper concluded, as did many others, that his memoirs "will be very widely read and will do infinite mischief."[1] While other reviewers offered more charitable assessments, most denounced the book (Documents 1–2).

The *Times* was proven correct on the first count: Barnum's autobiography, though met with ambivalence or even bafflement by many reviewers, became one of the bestselling books in American history. It went through at least seven editions in the United States alone and sold over a million copies, though Barnum reckoned that between both domestic and foreign editions—and the numerous cheap editions he handed out to visitors to his circus extravaganzas—the total readership probably topped four million. Regardless of the exact number of copies, the autobiography was one of the most widely read books in the United States in the second half of the nineteenth century outside of that perennial bestseller, the Bible.[2]

Whether Barnum's book did "infinite mischief" is another matter. Certainly, it sparked much controversy and more than a little unease. Its cavalier, picaresque account of how the great showman made money from exhibiting frauds, freaks, and curiosities of all kinds left some reviewers offended. Yet as the *Times* implied, what may have been most troubling was the fact that Barnum's life made a mockery of age-old advice governing the making of money. It seemed a complete repudiation of the lessons promulgated in that other bestselling primer for business success, Benjamin Franklin's *Autobiography*, which held up patience, self-discipline, and productive labor as the only reliable road to riches.

Here, by contrast, was a man who mocked the virtues of manual labor, recalling of his childhood that my father insisted that "I could hoe and plough and dig in the garden as well as anybody else, but I generally contrived to shirk the work altogether." Here was a gambler, not a plodder—a man who moved restlessly from one improbable enterprise to another, always with an eye on the main chance. "My disposition is, and ever was, of a speculative character," he mused in his memoirs, and his admission of this fact—indeed, celebration of it—struck many of the era's self-appointed guardians of virtue as heresy. If Franklin served as the ultimate embodiment of the "Protestant ethic," Barnum represented something entirely different and dangerous to many reviewers: an amoral, shape-shifting economic man.[3]

Yet a closer reading of Barnum's autobiography reveals someone far more complex and interesting than the one-sided caricatures sketched by early reviewers. Barnum was in fact a well-respected entrepreneur, and his famous lecture on the "Art of Money Getting"—as well as many sections of his *Life*—contain some of the same advice that can be found in Benjamin Franklin's equally influential life story. Sobriety, thrift, punctuality, honor, and all the other cardinal virtues of business success get their due in Barnum's memoirs. That these mingle so readily with a more speculative, impulsive life story is what makes the work distinctive—and representative. Though Franklin's life story offered a model of what Americans should be, Barnum's was closer in spirit to what many were in reality.[4]

In fact, for many people—especially foreigners—Barnum seemed the quintessential American. He embodied the brash, brazen qualities ascribed to Americans generally, particularly their sharp business dealings and talent for acquiring wealth in new and extraordinary ways. In the late 1830s and 1840s, it became commonplace to refer to American entrepreneurs as members of the "Universal Yankee Nation," a phrase laden with grudging admiration and a whiff of disgust. "Wherever money is to be made," wrote a British author who helped coin the phrase in 1838, "there are they as sure to be gathered together as young eagles over a carcass." Barnum was a bona fide citizen of this imagined polity, and he pointedly dedicated his memoirs to the "Universal Yankee Nation," adding, "of which, I am proud to be one."[5]

All of this is reason enough to read Barnum's autobiography. But it is the particular vocation Barnum pursued that makes him doubly fascinating. Barnum made his money by an almost alchemical process, turning things with no immediate commercial value into immensely profitable forms of mass entertainment. The raw material of Barnum's enterprises was eclectic and improbable: an elderly slave masquerading as George Washington's nursemaid, a grotesque monkey's head grafted onto the body of a fish, a mischievous dwarf child. Barnum turned them all into enormously profitable attractions, and he repeated the trick with endless variations throughout his long and eventful life. Sometimes his ventures were eminently respectable, such as his promotion of the Swedish opera singer Jenny Lind or the circus extravaganzas he staged later in his career. More often, though, his shows betrayed a touch of fraud, pretense, or just plain puffery.

The publication of the *Life of P. T. Barnum*, with its many revelations of chicanery, helped cement Barnum's reputation as a purveyor of "humbug," an all-purpose phrase used to describe what was spurious, if immensely entertaining, about Barnum's attractions. But humbug was the heart of something bigger. Barnum built his empire using methods that would become standard features of modern capitalism: marketing, advertising, and public relations. He was one of the first people to grasp that how you sold something was no less important than what you sold—and perhaps more important. Barnum's pioneering use of these promotional methods enabled him to play the role, as historian James Cook has put it, of "architect of the modern culture industry." His legacy in this respect is astonishing. Much of what now defines modern mass culture—celebrities, gossip, spin, and sensation—can trace its ancestry back to Barnum's original exhibits and entertainments. So, too, can the global reach of American popular culture, which in Barnum's hands became a valuable and enduring export, with Barnum himself the most recognizable "brand" of all.[6]

In short, it's next to impossible to grasp the nature of American capitalism—much less American culture—without revisiting Barnum. But all of this significance begs an obvious question: How did Barnum come to exercise such influence? How did a man of modest origins become, like his entertainments, a household name throughout the English-speaking world and beyond? The answer lies in part with his unusual childhood.

A CONNECTICUT YANKEE

Though many nineteenth-century reviewers assumed Barnum came from poverty, he was raised in a modestly prosperous family in the small village of Bethel, Connecticut. His father, a farmer and storekeeper, did die insolvent when Barnum was sixteen, but otherwise Barnum portrayed his childhood as idyllic. In fact, he devoted more pages to chronicling his early years than any other period, something that irked reviewers. One lamented that the first hundred-plus pages of the book "contain but little of the author's own history. They are almost entirely a rehearsal of "practical jokes" and smart sayings. . . ." Barnum anticipated this criticism. "I was born and reared in an atmosphere of merriment," he wrote by way of explanation, "and I feel myself entitled to record the sayings and doings of the wags and eccentricities of Bethel, because they partly explain the causes which have made me what I am."[7]

Of all the people in Barnum's childhood, his maternal grandfather, Phineas Taylor, loomed the largest, exercising an influence far greater than his own parents. Barnum recalled how "I was his pet, and spent probably the larger half of my waking hours in his arms, during the first six years of my life." Taylor was a prosperous landowner, justice of the peace, Revolutionary War veteran, state legislator, and town elder, but these markers of status and success belied a lighter, mirthful side. Barnum recalled that his grandfather "would go farther, wait longer, work harder and contrive deeper, to carry out a practical joke, than for anything else under heaven."[8]

This was no exaggeration. In one memorable episode, Barnum, his grandfather, and other men from Bethel boarded a sailing sloop bound for New York City. The trip could take as little as a day, but the wind did not cooperate. As the passengers sat on the becalmed ship, the lack of a razor left all of them with several days' growth of facial hair. Taylor, who alone had the foresight to bring a razor, agreed to loan it to his fellow passengers, all of who were desperate to appear their best when they walked off the ship. But he imposed a peculiar condition: Each man must shave half his face, leaving the other half hirsute. Only when the razor had made the rounds on the first half could they shave the rest of their faces. To this the other passengers reluctantly agreed, no doubt chalking this up to Taylor's fondness for merriment. Barnum described how this left all the men looking most ridiculous, though almost everyone joined in the laughter at seeing each other's half-shaven face.

But then Taylor took the joke to a higher level. After the razor circled back to Barnum's grandfather, he shaved the other half of his face—and then, with "well-feigned surprise," dropped the razor overboard. The other passengers, incredulous, realized they would shortly disembark in New York City with half-shaven faces. Taylor nonetheless persuaded his fellow villagers to adopt serious expressions as they marched to their hotel, ostensibly to avoid attracting attention from passing crowds. In reality, this was a set-up for yet another prank. At the hotel, he ordered drinks for the men as if nothing was amiss, and when bystanders demanded an explanation, he scolded them for staring, explaining that a half-shaven face was the "prevailing fashion" back in Bethel. The men, happy to play along in the latest iteration of the joke, sat with great solemnity in the bar, making Taylor's preposterous claim seem credible. As Barnum observed later in his autobiography, "a joke was never given up in Bethel until the very end of it was unraveled."[9]

These and other elaborate charades baffled some readers. Why go to such lengths to perpetrate a practical joke? The answer, Barnum made clear, was that the jokes often served a much deeper, very serious function. Barnum's memoirs suggest that these pranks often aimed to humble people who suffered from an exaggerated sense of their own importance or respectability. In the case of Taylor's shaving trick, one of the passengers, a prim preacher who sought to keep "aloof" from the men from Bethel, seems to have played this role. Elsewhere in the *Life*, equally self-important men—a learned lawyer, a "sanctimonious clergymen," and others—endured similar fates at the hands of Bethel's tricksters. The practical joke, then, had a most important function: It promoted equality. Anyone who put on airs would be taken down a notch.

This skepticism of authority reflected the radical changes taking place throughout much of American society at that time. In the decades following the American Revolution, longstanding social hierarchies began to crumble, particularly for ordinary white men. Barnum, the historian Neil Harris has observed, "grew up in an age of irreverence," when Americans "challenged notions of social order that had remained inviolate for centuries." This was an age that witnessed the abolition of property qualifications to vote, the eclipse of established religions by evangelical sects, and the emergence of a new kind of raucous democracy that put tremendous faith in the wisdom of the "common man." It is no accident that Barnum described himself and his family as ardent Democrats, foot soldiers in Andrew Jackson's political revolution.[10]

But it was the larger economic transformations of the era that did the most to destroy the older emphasis on deference and hierarchy that had knit together American society in the decades before Barnum's birth. Over the course of Barnum's lifetime, a far more rough-and-tumble, aggressive brand of economic striving took root and flourished. Barnum, one insightful historian has argued, "lived in an era of unbridled competition among men who acknowledged no betters. He came of age amid the liberal scramble and the capitalist clamor that Franklin only forecast." As the headlong pursuit of wealth became commonplace and even respectable in the Jacksonian era, the self-made man of business soon supplanted the landed aristocrat as the ideal to which young men should strive.[11]

The emergent ethos of self-making likely informed the most controversial prank that Barnum's grandfather perpetrated, with his grandson playing the dupe. Barnum related the story in his autobiography and frequently recounted it in public lectures. It seems to have been one of the most important, formative experiences of his childhood. As Barnum recalled, from the time he turned four years old, his beloved grandfather—as well as his parents and all the townspeople—began telling him that he would one day inherit a valuable tract of land called Ivy Island some miles away from home. Barnum heard much of this land, which he imagined "the most valuable farm in Connecticut," and he daydreamed of the day when it would become his own, making him wealthier than the other children his age. Barnum begged to see Ivy Island for years, and when he turned twelve his family relented, though they cautioned him not to let the splendor of his patrimony go to his head. But when Barnum finally glimpsed Ivy Island, he beheld nothing more than a few acres of barren, snake-infested land in the middle of a stream. At that moment, "all my visions of future wealth and greatness vanished into thin air," Barnum recalled in his autobiography.[12]

Yet the revelation hardly destroyed Barnum's confidence. Instead, he seems to have drawn precisely the lessons that his family intended, abandoning his childish pretensions to greatness. Without the safety net of a landed inheritance, Barnum prepared to make his way in the world on the strength of his own abilities. As an adult, he passed along this lesson to young men who wished to succeed in business. "Do not depend on others," he wrote. "Your success must depend upon your own individual exertions. . . . learn that every man must be the architect of his own fortune." In typical fashion, though, Barnum managed to have the last laugh with regard to Ivy Island, putting it up as collateral for a business loan that underwrote his purchase of the American Museum (Document 3), the building that became the centerpiece of his entertainment empire.[13]

In other ways, too, the pranks and jokes that Barnum watched and witnessed prepared him for success in an unforgiving business world. In the nineteenth-century marketplace, the ethic of *caveat emptor*—buyer beware—increasingly dominated commerce, and Barnum's region of the country had an especially notorious reputation for taking no prisoners in the pursuit of profit. One British visitor from the 1820s recalled that Americans all agreed that New England's people "present a spectacle of industry and prosperity delightful to behold" at the same time they universally portrayed them as "sly, grinding, selfish, and tricking." Worse, the New Englanders "will avow these qualities themselves with a complacent smile, and boast that no people on the earth can match them at overreaching in a bargain." This could readily describe Barnum's Bethel, never mind the tone of the autobiography itself.[14]

The constant tricks, jokes, and pranks that defined Barnum's childhood thus offered a valuable preparation for the real world, where every economic transaction was a battle of wits and a test of wills. All the antics of Barnum's upbringing may have been amusing, but they also ensured Barnum rarely ended up the loser in the commercial gambles of his adult years. The autobiography is replete with instances where Barnum outwits competitors, double-crossers, and cheats seeking to best the showman. Much of the credit for his success in defeating these adversaries must lie with the training he received at the hands of Phineas Taylor and his fellow pranksters. The now familiar phrase "it takes a village" assumes a whole new meaning in the context of Barnum's life.

If Barnum's childhood made him watchful and wary, it did not make him cynical. In a telling introduction to another book he published, *Humbugs of the World* (Document 12), Barnum wrote, "the greatest humbug of all is the man who believes—or pretends to believe—that everything and everybody are humbugs. We sometimes meet a person who professes that there is no virtue; that every man has his price, and every woman hers. . . ." Anyone so constituted, Barnum thundered, was like a "hog's mind in a man's body—sensual, greedy, selfish, cruel, cunning, sly . . ." Such a man, Barnum declared, "instead of showing that others are rotten inside . . . has proved that he is," and that when "he sneers, full of deceit and nastiness—it is his own foul breath that he smells." Such a man, Barnum argued, was not merely despicable. Nor was he worth of being called a "humbug." He was nothing more than a "fool."[15]

This bit of stern moralizing, coming from a man who often tried the patience of his contemporaries, seems odd. But Barnum's own private writings suggest that he took grave offense at charges that he was a hardnosed peddler of fraud. He readily conceded that at times he had stretched "the cords of morality" in order to further some practical joke or other scheme. But he did so in order to entertain, and in his own mind at least, the ends justified the means. So long as his audience felt they had gotten their money's worth, what did it matter if deception and trickery had played a role? Barnum thus resurrected the rituals of his rural childhood for adult city dwellers, making a fortune in the process. As he concluded in his autobiography, "the public appears disposed to be amused even when they are conscious of being deceived."

Indeed, many audience members enjoyed the hoaxes and pranks that Barnum staged. His impostures, one historian has observed, found such a congenial reception because prior to Barnum, no one "had ever taken the pains to delude them on so preposterous a scale." Moreover, they offered a role for the audience, one that empowered them to make the final judgment. "Barnum's audiences found the encounter with potential frauds exciting," another scholar has noted. "It was a form of intellectual exercise, stimulating even when literal truth could not be determined." The showman's defenders understood this and did not shy away from hitting back at self-righteous critics. As the *Knickerbocker Magazine* declared after reading Barnum's autobiography, "it has been common enough with thousands to denounce Mr. Barnum as a 'humbug,' and with this contemptuous term to dismiss his name from conversation. But for our part, we wish there were more just such 'humbugs' in the world."[16]

In Barnum's hands fraud could be more than entertaining; it could be instructive, as audience members accepted the challenge of sorting out the fake from the real—and plenty was real. Much of what awaited visitors to the American Museum was entirely authentic, if occasionally curious: sideshow curiosities, such as Siamese twins, bearded ladies, dwarves, and giants; a range of art work, including portraits, statutes, and paintings; a theater where Barnum staged plays, musical performances, and lectures; all manner of exotic animals and birds, some alive and some stuffed; fossils, gems, and other natural history specimens; and many other genuine attractions. As this same reviewer noted, "we wish there were a few more such places as the 'American Museum,' where attractive amusement and valuable information could be so liberally and cheaply furnished."[17]

There was some truth to this assessment. Barnum's American Museum was one of the few places—perhaps the only place—in New York City where such a broad cross-section of citizens came together. Though leery of the more boisterous working-class men who lived in the nearby Bowery neighborhood, Barnum worked hard to banish class distinctions, creating the illusion of a democratic space in an otherwise heavily divided city. Certainly, the twenty-five cents he charged for admission excluded the city's poorest citizens, but anyone willing to pay this modest price gained access to the same exhibits and entertainments, regardless of their social status. Moreover, Barnum worked hard to ensure that women, especially single women, could attend the museum without fear of harassment. He enforced a strict code of conduct on visitors, even going so far as to hire private detectives to patrol the building, escorting anyone who misbehaved out to the street. The American Museum was, despite Barnum's reputation for humbug, an eminently respectable institution that catered to a more diverse audience than most of the era's entertainments.[18]

Yet there was a more troubling aspect to Barnum's attractions, one that drew little attention at the time. Modern readers coming to Barnum's autobiography for the first time may not find the hoaxes all that disturbing. But they are likely to come away disquieted over his exploitation of African Americans.

THE SHOWMAN AND SLAVERY

Barnum shared the casual racism that pervaded antebellum American society. In much of his public and private writings from this period, he comes across as largely indifferent to the plight of blacks, free or enslaved. As the abolitionist movement gathered steam from the 1830s onward, Barnum remained disengaged. In one typical missive from 1845, he declared, "I am no apologist for slavery, and I abhor its existence as much as any man. But the rabid fanaticism of some abolitionists is more reprehensible than slavery itself and only serves to strengthen instead of weaken the fetters of the enslaved."

Like many of Barnum's statements, though, this one stretched the truth. When Barnum took a motley collection of performers on a tour of the South in the late 1830s, he apparently purchased a slave to serve as his valet. When the man allegedly stole money from Barnum, the showman whipped him and sold him at auction in New Orleans. Barnum also seems to have accepted a slave women and child as a form of payment when settling up at the end of the trip. He promptly sold both in the slave markets of St. Louis.[19]

Barnum's opportunistic relationship with slavery was perhaps typical of many Northerners, few of whom actively opposed the institution and in some cases even profited from it. But Barnum's connection to the "peculiar institution," as slavery was called, went farther than these episodes. In fact, his very first success as a showman was the exhibition of Joice Heth, an elderly slave whom he leased from her owner. Heth claimed she had served as George Washington's nursemaid, raising the future president from birth onward. Barnum trumpeted these claims—along with sometimes grotesque, racist descriptions of Heth's appearance—in a relentless advertising campaign. He invited audiences to visit what he called a "marvelous relic of antiquity" who, at an alleged 161 years of age, offered a spectacle that could appeal to the patriotic and voyeuristic alike.

Like his grandfather's elaborate practical jokes, Barnum's exhibition of Heth went through many stages, each of which drew new audiences. When Barnum displayed Heth in the abolitionist stronghold of Providence, Rhode Island, the local clergy assailed the exhibit as exploitative. As attendance declined, Barnum planted stories in the local press claiming that Heth was free and that proceeds from the exhibit would go toward emancipating her great-grandchildren who remained in slavery. Once again, ticket sales went up and Barnum reaped the rewards. When Heth died in 1836, Barnum managed to extract yet more money from the slave by sponsoring an autopsy of her body. Upward of 1,500 people paid Barnum 50 cents apiece to view the show, a spectacle ostensibly meant to determine her true age. The eminent surgeon David Rogers played the part of the forensic examiner, dismembering Heth's body before the rapt crowd. Rogers concluded that Heth was not more than eighty, and Barnum allegedly buried the body—or what was left of it—in his hometown of Bethel. The grave has never been found, prompting some historians to wonder whether Barnum gave Heth the dignity of a proper burial.[20]

For much of the 1850s, Barnum continued to rely on racist entertainments to turn a profit. He promoted blackface minstrelsy, a form of popular entertainment where white performers would caricature African Americans in songs and skits. He also created an exhibit called "What Is It?" that featured an African American man with an abnormally sloped cranium (Documents 7–10). Though this unknown performer was an ordinary person with a misshapen head, Barnum had him fitted with a fur suit and put on display. Barnum told the public that he had captured him in Africa and fanned speculation that he was a "missing link," playing off racial theories that portrayed blacks as a separate race as well as the recent publication of Charles Darwin's *On the Origin of Species*. At the same time, he steadfastly ignored the rising tide of antislavery sentiment. When Harriet Beecher Stowe's stridently abolitionist novel *Uncle Tom's Cabin* became a bestselling book in 1853, Barnum staged an unauthorized theatrical adaption that neutered Stowe's radical message. The abolitionist *New-York Tribune* panned Barnum's production, condemning it as a "play to which no apologist for Slavery could object." Nor did Barnum welcome African Americans to the entertainments that he promoted during this time.[21]

And yet Barnum, like many Americans, eventually adopted more liberal views on the question of slavery and race. After Southerners tried to force slavery on the territories of Kansas and Nebraska, Barnum became disillusioned with the Democratic Party. His wife Charity, who played a large if invisible role in shaping Barnum's political views, had already converted to the antislavery cause. By the late 1850s, Barnum followed her lead. He joined the Republican Party, and the entertainments at the American Museum reflected a newly enlightened view. He replaced the old production of *Uncle Tom's Cabin* with a far more faithful adaptation; he also staged a theatrical production of Stowe's antislavery sequel, *Dred*. In 1860, he voted for Abraham Lincoln and became a stalwart defender of the Union cause and an increasingly vocal foe of slavery even as racism remained central to some of his entertainments.[22]

While it's tempting to read Barnum's conversion as nothing more than a response to changing public opinion, it's important to remember that New York City, where Barnum staged most of his entertainments, was deeply hostile to Lincoln and to the Republican Party, never mind abolition. It was, one historian has observed, "the most southern of northern cities," a dangerous place to be a rabid Unionist. And yet Barnum used the American Museum throughout the war to showcase his Unionist bona fides, including patriotic exhibits, lectures, and shows. Barnum's dedication to the Union cause was unwavering throughout the war. In fact, when Southern saboteurs sought to burn down land-marks in New York City, they rather tellingly targeted Barnum's American Museum first—without success.[23]

Barnum's growing disgust with slavery informed his decision to run for a seat in the Connecticut state legislature in 1865. Motivated, he later recalled, by a desire to cast a vote in favor of the Thirteenth Amendment to the Constitution (which abolished slavery), Barnum won election as a Republican. He distinguished himself as a state legislator, but as one of his biographers has noted, his finest moment likely came when he delivered a speech in 1865 in favor of an amendment to the Connecticut state constitution that would have given blacks the right to vote. That passionate speech reflected a remarkable evolution in Barnum's thinking, as did comments he made at a political rally two years later. "I lived [in the South] and owned slaves," he confessed to the audience. "I did more. I whipped my slaves. I ought to have been whipped a thousand times for this myself."[24]

Though willing to reckon with his complicity in this instance, Barnum's disgust with slavery did not translate into a full-fledged vision of racial equality. Racist jokes and caricatures infused popular culture, and Barnum happily catered to popular taste. Yet if Barnum may not have been a radical when it came to race relations, he expressed convictions that were, for their time, relatively progressive. "No intelligent observer can fail to be struck by the aptitude of those of African descent for the acquisition of knowledge," he wrote toward the end of his life, singling out in particular "the readiness with which they assimilate good business ideas." This was high praise: business was what Barnum knew best.[25]

BARNUM THE BUSINESSMAN

When historians write about Barnum, they focus on his penchant for stretching the truth, or on occasion, peddling outright falsehoods. It is certainly what drew the attention of some many reviewers and readers of the autobiography, many of whom professed themselves shocked by Barnum's duplicity, never mind his willingness to share these secrets. "It was a bold experiment to come out and tell the world that his long career had been a series of cheats and humbugs, and that he had made a handsome fortune by it," sniffed one reviewer in 1855.[26]

These responses conveniently ignored the fact that Barnum was hardly alone in engaging in such trickery. If Barnum had committed a sin, it seems to have been the honesty with which he related the story behind some of his more famous impostures. Moreover, compared to many of the confidence men and scam artists who populated the economic landscape at this time, Barnum's practical jokes on the public seem pretty tame, particularly given that people happily paid money—sometimes over and over—to see them. By contrast, the more troubling faces of fraud in this era—patent-medicine salesmen who peddled sugar water to people dying of disease, swindlers who robbed the ignorant of their life's savings, and other figures who preyed upon the vulnerable—arguably fell into a different category. Genuine confidence men preyed on the unwary masses; Barnum merely entertained them—or so he claimed.

The focus on fraud in Barnum's career also blinds us to the fact that he was, at heart, a sophisticated businessman, not a fly-by-night charlatan. As one of Barnum's most insightful biographers has written, the great showman was "neither a good-natured deceiver nor an evil-minded philistine, but an intelligent, complex, and well-organized entrepreneur whose business involved the myths and values of a self-proclaimed democracy." He may have been a particularly flamboyant member of this class of capitalist strivers, but Barnum had plenty of company. His life story helps illuminate the chaotic, often unforgiving capitalist economy of the nineteenth century, which left behind as many spectacular failures as it did uplifting stories of success. Barnum would endure and enjoy both these fates over the course of his lifetime.[27]

Many of the era's entrepreneurs had their hands in a bewildering range of ventures and schemes, and Barnum was no exception. By the time the first edition of the autobiography appeared, Barnum had opened a porter house, or saloon, in Brooklyn and multiple country stores in Connecticut; sold lottery tickets and launched lotteries of his own; published and edited a newspaper; tried his hand at making and selling boot blacking, bear grease, and cologne; and managed a host of exhibits that launched his career as a showman. He built a palace of entertainment in New York City called the American Museum; thousands of people visited it every day. In the early 1850s, Barnum became a concert promoter, too, turning the Swedish opera singer Jenny Lind into an international sensation. He dabbled in land speculation, banking, and many other secondary enterprises.

By 1852, Barnum was one of the most visible and successful entrepreneurs in the nation. When a Philadelphia author named Edwin Freedley compiled a primer of advice on how to succeed in business, he predictably solicited Barnum to share the secrets of his success. Barnum happily complied, and Freedley published Barnum's essay verbatim, proudly showcasing the advice of a man he called "one of the most successful business men of the age." Yet the advice itself was largely uncontroversial. Indeed, much of it could have come from that other patron saint of businessmen at the time, Benjamin Franklin. Barnum admonished his readers to follow a version of what has since become known as the Protestant ethic: a code of moral and economic behavior that puts a premium on frugality, hard work, and self-discipline in order to get ahead in the world. He counseled readers to defer gratification and "avoid extravagance" and extolled the "pleasure of saving." Many of the newly wealthy, he warned, "immediately commence expending for luxuries until in a short time their expenses swallow up their income." He advised readers to avoid "visionary" schemes and emphasized the importance of self-discipline and self-reliance and the supreme importance of keeping one's commercial promises: "nothing is more valuable to a man in business than the name of always doing as he agrees, and that to the moment." And not surprisingly, he admonished readers to "use no description of intoxicating drinks" and urged them to work "with all your might . . . never deferring for a single hour that which can just as well be done *now*."[28]

Given Barnum's reputation for saying one thing and doing another, it may come as a surprise to learn that much of this advice was rooted in his own habits. His work ethic was legendary: He hated manual labor, but when he sought to turn a speculation to success, he followed the advice he gave his readers: "work at it if necessary early and late, in season and out of season, not leaving a stone unturned." Moreover, Barnum was a devout Christian: "I always attended church regularly," he declared in his memoirs, and when traveling, "was never without a Bible." His religious worldview informed his crusade against alcohol, and by the 1850s, Barnum had become a strident temperance advocate, delivering lectures on the evils of drink. And while he may have left some of his customers feeling shortchanged, he enjoyed a solid reputation for honesty in his business partnerships.[29]

Nonetheless, it was one thing to endorse a code of business conduct; it was altogether another thing to actually abide by it. Like many of his fellow entrepreneurs, Barnum had difficulty taking his own advice. He hardly eschewed extravagance, building himself a wildly ornate "Oriental villa" in Bridgeport, Connecticut, that he grandly dubbed "Iranistan" (Document 4). With over fifty rooms and many acres of manicured gardens and outbuilding, Barnum's new home was a monument to his own success. "The inside is finished and furnished in the most costly and tasteful manner," reported one newspaper, "far superior to any country seat in the United States, if not the world." While Barnum's estate did not proclaim his superiority to the masses—rather than walling himself off from the public, he encouraged people to stroll the grounds—Iranistan's over-the-top ostentation flagrantly contradicted the precepts of frugality and restraint that he held up as essential to business success.[30]

And while Barnum urged readers to "engage in one kind of business only," he could not resist speculating in ventures where he had little experience. He eventually flew too close to the sun. After moving to Bridgeport, Barnum poured vast amounts of money into what became known as East Bridgeport, which he hoped to turn into an industrial hub midway between New Haven and New York. This led to real estate speculation and an ever-growing portfolio of investments and enterprises. He even founded a financial institution—the Pequonnock Bank—and served as its president. In 1852, Barnum lured a clock manufacturing company to East Bridgeport, which was reborn as the Terry and Barnum Manufacturing Company. Then, in 1855, he struck a deal with the Jerome Manufacturing Company, a maker of high-quality brass clocks. Barnum extended his own credit to the company, putting up Iranistan and his other personal property as collateral. In exchange, the clock company's owner, Chauncey Jerome, agreed to move his factory to East Bridgeport and merge it with Barnum's clock company.

Barnum, who represented much of what was wild and untamed about American capitalism, had now, in a rather ironic turn of events, bet his entire fortune on the consummate symbol of order and predictability in the emerging industrial economy: the clock. It was an improbable investment, and it soon went terribly awry. After sinking immense amounts of money into Jerome's business, Barnum belatedly discovered that the funds he put up went to paying off debts that the clockmaker incurred before partnering with Barnum. In short time, Barnum became the target of the failing company's creditors, and he found himself on the hook for over half a million dollars in debt. When the Jerome Manufacturing Company went bankrupt in February 1856, Barnum followed suit. He was forced to relinquish all his property, moving into rented quarters in New York City. For the remainder of the year, Barnum's creditors hounded him in bankruptcy court, convinced that the wily showman had managed to shield his assets.[31]

Over the course of 1856, the nation watched in disbelief as Barnum's empire crumbled. More than a few lamented his bankruptcy: Barnum, for all the controversy he stirred, had been a much-beloved figure in popular culture, and the improbable reasons for his failure—a bad investment in clocks?—garnered him some sympathy. But for a handful of observers, the impulse to moralize proved hard to resist. One newspaper claimed that a mere year after Barnum had portrayed himself as the "Prince of Cheats" who had built "an immense fortune" on fraudulent foundations, "the Humbug has been humbugged out of his gains by greater Humbugs than himself." All of this struck this author as a "righteous retribution" and unassailable proof that "God is just." The *New York Herald* likewise declared that Barnum's spectacular collapse was "a case eminently adapted to point a moral or adorn a tale." The *Herald* concluded that Barnum would now vanish and that "the poison of that demoralizing book"—the autobiography—"is thus effectively rendered innocuous. It can do no further harm." The following year, Barnum's beloved Iranistan burned to the ground, punctuating his fall from grace.[32]

Barnum's failure, though especially spectacular and visible, was hardly unusual. Many of the era's entrepreneurs saw their hard-won fortunes destroyed when the intricate webs of credit and debt that bound them together unraveled. Some became disconsolate at their ill fortune, but Barnum took a strange solace from his fate. "I am being taught humility and reliance upon Providence," he wrote one of his business partners at this time. "The man who coins his brain and blood into gold, who wastes all of his time and thought upon the almighty dollar . . . and whose iron chest is crammed with stocks and mortgages tied up with his own heartstrings, may console himself with the idea of safe investments, but he misses a pleasure which I firmly believe this lesson was intended to secure to me." Barnum sincerely believed his bankruptcy was heaven sent. He would learn to be "patient and submissive" in adjusting to his fate.

He retreated to the seashore with his wife and three daughters, taking refuge in feminine company as his creditors continued to pick over his estate. During this period, he later wrote, "I found more peace & contentment than Iranistan ever afforded me." As he contemplated his fate, though, Barnum had no intention of submitting to a life of penury. Rather, he interpreted his failure as a message to change his ways rather than change his vocation. He began to negotiate with his creditors, leaning on his wife Charity, whose own assets he deployed in his bid for redemption. (Barnum, always quick with a pun, liked to tell friends "without charity, I am nothing.") The business community of Bridgeport also lent a hand, having long depended on Barnum's philanthropy, credit, and showmanship to put their city on the map. They held meetings in support of Barnum's efforts, and many business associates intervened on his behalf. By the end of 1856, Barnum's precarious situation had stabilized, though he still owed a staggering amount of money to his many creditors.[33]

In 1857, he launched a slow and deliberate campaign to rise from the ashes. He traveled to London, where friends urged him to make some foray into public life. He began crafting a lecture on what he called "The Art of Money Getting," though he joked that he would do better to give talks on "The Art of Money Losing." This presentation, drawn from his original essay in Freedley's *A Treatise on Business*, added wisdom wrung from bankruptcy. He was speaking from experience when he warned, "never let a man foolishly jeopardize a fortune that he has earned in a legitimate way, by investing it in things in which he has had no experience." Equally personal, given his entanglement with Jerome, was his declaration that one should never guarantee another man's debt without adequate security. And while his advice to avoid extravagance could come across as a bit hypocritical, it was almost certainly more heartfelt at this stage in Barnum's career. Thanks to his charismatic delivery, Barnum received rave reviews when he first gave the lecture. He then went on a speaking tour throughout Britain and its possessions, delivering the same speech over sixty more times. He amassed a small fortune in the process, enabling him to retire some of his debts. In the process, Barnum began to reclaim his empire from his creditors. By 1860, he had resumed ownership of the American Museum, discharging his remaining debts. Though he would once again accumulate vast wealth, Barnum never again built the equivalent of Iranistan. Nor did he dabble in ventures outside his competency.[34]

In 1869, Barnum released an updated version of his memoirs. In a nod to his catastrophic bankruptcy and his eventual redemption, he gave it a new, telling title: *Struggles and Triumphs*.[35]

BARNUM'S LEGACY

Barnum transformed popular culture in the United States. He pioneered genres of mass entertainment aimed at the broad, deep, and difficult-to-define swath of society known as the middle class. His productions consequently attracted an enormous audience. Barnum's American Museum alone welcomed almost 38 million visitors between 1841 and 1865. His traveling three-ring circus and other spectacular staged extravaganzas entertained many millions more (Document 13). "I have amused and instructed more persons than any other manager who ever lived," wrote Barnum toward the end of his life, without exaggeration.[36]

The scale of Barnum's audience ensured that he would have a hand in shaping the worldview of several generations of Americans. This was especially the case with his many attractions that highlighted the exotic, the foreign, and the "primitive." These attractions, which Barnum packaged as a mix of education and entertainment, included a "Chinese Museum" in New York that featured a Chinese woman and her family, alleged cannibals from Fiji, and numerous other exhibits, all part of what Barnum promoted at various times as either a "Human Menagerie" or a "Congress of Nations." Half human zoo, half natural history museum, these living exhibits, complete with native dress, strange rituals, and musical performances, gave audiences a sense, however inaccurate, of the wider world. All of them affirmed and amplified existing prejudices and stereotypes and invariably put white Americans atop a racial hierarchy. As the United States rose to global dominance by the end of the century, Barnum's entertainments became object lessons for Americans eager to establish empires on par with those founded by European powers.[37]

Barnum's influence on American culture was more benign—and enduring. While it would be naïve to believe that Barnum somehow managed to draw all of American society to his many attractions, he did manage to create a more democratic, inclusive brand of entertainment than generally existed at this time. Ordinary working people, eminent intellectuals, foreign nobility, and middle-class office workers all attended Barnum's American Museum and, later, his circus extravaganzas. Barnum, of course, never had any high-minded desire to bring together people of dissimilar backgrounds under the same roof or, later, the same big tent. He simply wanted to attract as many patrons as possible: The more visitors, the more money he would make. But this philosophy—that popular culture with the broadest possible audience held the promise of the greatest profits—continues to drive the entertainment business today, even in the twenty-first century, when "niche" audiences are commonplace.

Barnum also transformed the relationship between his audiences and the attractions of mass culture. Though some of Barnum's entertainments encouraged passivity, particularly his later, spectacular circus extravaganzas, many more invited the public to entertain itself. He began this process in 1854, staging the nation's first beauty pageant. This sparked controversy—respectable ladies refused to participate— and Barnum found a more congenial way to stage the event. He invited women to submit photographs of themselves, posted them at his museum, and then invited the public to vote on the winner. This was a success, as were his famous "baby shows" held the following year, which invited mothers to enter their infants in contests, with prizes given to the "finest" and "fattest" babies, among other distinctions. These shows, which attracted great interest and controversy, offered the opportunity for ordinary people to find fame. They are the direct antecedents of today's reality television shows and programs like *American Idol*.[38]

Barnum's legacy goes far beyond these examples. On a much deeper level, he helped make advertising, marketing, and public relations acceptable, if not respectable. He understood far better that success in business rested on more than the quality of a product or service; it was necessary to attract customers. The location of a business mattered, a point he hammered home in his popular lecture on making money. But so, too, did advertising. All of his promotions depended on what was then a staggering amount of money spent on newspapers advertising as well as placards, handbills, and other printed ephemera that promoted his shows and exhibits. Barnum inundated the public with advertising. He did not stint on this investment, and his memoirs chronicle his many successes using the generative powers of "printer's ink."

Advertising could take many forms. When Barnum bought the American Museum, he inherited a plain and unremarkable building. He later wrote that "there was no bustle or activity about the place; no posters to announce what was to be seen; — the whole exterior was as dead as the skeletons and stuffed skins within." In short order Barnum transformed the building into the biggest advertisement of all, adding flags and banners depicting the wonders that awaited visitors. He then placed enormous limelights — lights that burned calcium oxide — atop the building, making the museum the brightest place in New York City. "These were the first [limelights] ever seen in New York," he recalled. "They made people talk, and so advertised my Museum."[39]

Barnum made advertising central to the advice he gave aspiring entrepreneurs in his writings on business success. "The business men of this country do not, as a general thing, appreciate the advantages of advertising thoroughly," he observed. This was foolish: "Advertise your business" was one of the cardinal precepts he gave aspiring entrepreneurs, adding that while "there may possibly be occupations that do not require advertising . . . I cannot well conceive what they are." For Barnum, there was no limit on the amount of money one could — and should — spend on advertising. He put the matter bluntly in his lecture on money making: "a man who advertises at all must keep it up until the public know who and what he is, and what his business is, or else the money invested in advertising is lost."[40]

It is hard to appreciate how unsettling this advice seemed when Barnum gave it. In the twenty-first century, advertising has become such a fixture of everyday life that it is strange to imagine a world without it. Advertising is its own industry, and advertisements can sometimes assume lives above and beyond the products they promote: Think of the half-time commercials of the Super Bowl, for example. But in Barnum's era, advertising struck many people as unnecessary, even duplicitous. Indeed, the industry best known for advertising in Barnum's lifetime was the patent-medicine business, which peddled bogus wares. But Barnum, who became extraordinarily adept at turning illusions into profits, understood how advertising could summon demand out of thin air. Writing of advertising's strange power in 1852, Barnum told the nation's entrepreneurs, "Put on the *appearance* of business, and generally the *reality* will follow."[41]

This philosophy animated much of what Barnum did beyond mere advertising. The showman understood that no exhibit, event, or attraction necessarily succeeded on its merits alone. It was necessary to massage and manipulate public attention via the media. Long before public relations became a field unto itself, Barnum grasped the symbiotic relationship between business and the press. While there is no evidence that Barnum claimed that "there is no such thing as bad publicity," the fact that this quote has so often been ascribed to him testifies to his lifelong reliance on the press to achieve his commercial ends. Barnum masterfully deployed the press in all of his early successes, from Joice Heth to the Feejee Mermaid.

By the late 1840s, Barnum had perfected these methods and taken them in new and revolutionary directions. At this time, people began using the word *celebrity* to mean someone famous or noteworthy. Unlike older definitions of fame, which was limited to well-known leaders, anyone could be a celebrity. And here Barnum played an important role. His first successful experiment with turning an unknown into a celebrity was his discovery and management of the child dwarf Charles Stratton. Barnum renamed him "General Tom Thumb," and after some musical and theatrical training, turned his young protégé into an international star (Document 5). After triumphal tours of Europe in the 1840s, Thumb was hounded by frenzied fans; his autograph became a sought-after prize, and the press followed his every move with fascination. Barnum ultimately capitalized on Thumb's popularity by arranging a celebrity wedding with another dwarf, an event that struck many as crass and tasteless but which, like so much of celebrity culture, proved endlessly entertaining[42] (Documents 11 and 12).

But Barnum's handling of the Swedish opera singer Jenny Lind arguably represented his greatest triumph in nurturing and profiting from celebrity. Though Lind "mania" had already seized Europe, Barnum took matters to an entirely new level when he signed a contract to manage her concert tour in the United States. It was a bold speculation, given that he had never heard her sing. In September 1850, he nonetheless "commenced preparing the public mind through the newspapers for the reception of the great songstress" after signing a contract with her. Barnum left nothing to chance. As he later recalled, he put "innumerable means and appliances into operation for the furtherance of my object, and little did the public see of the hand that indirectly pulled at their heart strings, preparatory to a relaxation of their purse-strings." Barnum gradually released heart-warming details of her life, focusing less on her actual musical abilities than her remarkable rise from obscurity to international stardom.

Barnum, who usually found a way to involve the public in his entertainments, launched a competition—complete with a cash prize—for the best "ode," which Lind would sing at the first concert. He oversaw the design of the concert tickets, the seating, and every other imaginable detail connected to Lind's impending tour. This was akin to a product launch in our own era, and Barnum's many contrivances paid off: By the time Lind arrived in New York City by ship, an immense crowd stood waiting to greet her, complete with banners, though Barnum managed this welcome as well, as his autobiography makes clear. To Barnum's critics, Lind's carefully contrived apotheosis as the "Swedish Nightingale" seemed a sham, the product of artful manipulations and clever marketing (Document 6). Barnum naturally disagreed.

Lind's arrival in the United States was but the beginning. Prior to her first concert, Barnum auctioned off some of the choicest tickets to the highest bidder, adding to the excitement. Throughout her tour, Barnum showered friendly editors with free tickets, ensuring media coverage at little cost. In fact, what was remarkable about Barnum's success with Lind was the extent to which he set this commercial juggernaut in motion without heavy reliance on traditional advertising. Additional entrepreneurs eager to cash in on Lind's popularity likely aided Barnum. Manufacturers of a range of consumer goods borrowed her image to hawk their wares. Barnum recalled that "We had Jenny Lind gloves, Jenny Lind bonnets, Jenny Lind riding hats, Jenny Lind shawls, mantillas, robes, chairs, sofas, pianos—in fact, every thing was

Jenny Lind." All of this merchandising put Lind before the public at no cost to Barnum.[43]

If Barnum's management of Lind marked the first time that he had wedded advertising, publicity, and celebrity into such a heady mix, there was yet another person whom he promoted to dizzying levels of fame and fortune: himself. Barnum became the ultimate celebrity, someone whose name recognition exceeded and outlasted his many performers and protégés. Indeed, Barnum's public persona, carefully crafted over many decades—and then disseminated through countless copies of the autobiography—may have been his greatest triumph of all, as some of his obituaries observed (Document 14).

In 1885, Barnum met former President Ulysses S. Grant, who had recently returned from a well-publicized trip around the world. In the final version of the autobiography, Barnum recounted how he congratulated Grant, telling him "since your journey around the world, you are the best known man on the globe." Grant demurred. "No sir," he told Barnum. "Your name is familiar to multitudes who never heard of me. Wherever I went, among the most distant nations, the fact that I was an American led to constant inquiries whether I knew Barnum." Barnum took great pleasure in this assessment, and a few weeks later, he received some proof that this was indeed the case. A letter arrived in the mail that had traveled from Burma. It was simply addressed "Mr. Barnum, America." It found its way to Bridgeport by way of Bombay, Brindisi, and several other cities, traveling halfway around the world to the showman's home—confirmation, he wrote, of "my name being known to the ends of the earth."[44]

By the time he died, Barnum was a household name throughout the world. He has since fallen out of favor, a fate that almost all celebrities eventually share. But his memoirs remain, an artifact no less curious or remarkable than the attractions that once filled the American Museum. Like that letter he received late in life, his autobiography is a missive from a distant land: the lost world of nineteenth-century America.

NOTES

[1]Phineas T. Barnum, *The Life of P. T. Barnum, Written by Himself* (New York: Redfield, 1855); "The Lesson of Barnum's Life," *New York Daily Times*, December 16, 1854, 4. On the well-publicized negotiations for the book, see Arthur H. Saxon, *P. T. Barnum: The Legend and the Man* (New York: Columbia University Press, 1989), 8–9.

[2]Carl Bode, who edited a later edition of Barnum's memoirs, argued that, aside from the Bible, it was the most widely read book in the second half of the nineteenth century.

See Carl Bode, ed., *Struggles and Triumphs: Or, Forty Years' Recollections of P. T. Barnum* (New York: Penguin, 1981), 23. Barnum's estimates appear in P. T. Barnum, *The Life of P. T. Barnum: Written by Himself, Including His Golden Rules for Money-Making, Brought Up to 1888* (Buffalo, NY: Courier Company, 1888), 314.

[3]Barnum, *Life of P. T. Barnum* (1855), 22, 107; Max Weber, *The Protestant Ethic and the Spirit of Capitalism*, trans. Talcott Parson (1904; New York: Routledge, 1992).

[4]A fascinating comparison of Franklin and Barnum can be found in Michael Zuckerman, *Almost Chosen People: Oblique Biographies in the American Grain* (Berkeley: University of California Press, 1993), 145–174.

[5]*London Quarterly Review*, June 1838, 194. On this term and its general use in the United States, see George C. Rable, *Damn Yankees!: Demonization and Defiance in the Confederate South* (Baton Rouge, LA: LSU Press, 2015).

[6]James W. Cook, ed., *The Colossal P. T. Barnum Reader: Nothing Else Like It in the Universe* (Urbana and Chicago: University of Illinois Press, 2005), 1; Bluford Adams, *E Pluribus Barnum: The Great Showman and the Making of U.S. Popular Culture* (Minneapolis: University of Minnesota Press, 1997).

[7]Barnum, *Life of P. T. Barnum* (1855), 105; "Barnum a Martyr!" *Ladies Repository*, March 1855, 170; Saxon, *P. T. Barnum*, 24–46.

[8]Barnum, *Life of P. T. Barnum* (1855), 10; Saxon, *P. T. Barnum*, 28–29.

[9]Barnum, *Life of P. T. Barnum* (1855), 55–61, 120.

[10]Neil Harris, *Humbug: The Art of P. T. Barnum* (Chicago: University of Chicago, 1975), 3. See also Gordon Wood, *The Radicalism of the American Revolution* (New York; Vintage, 1991); Joyce Appleby, *Inheriting the Revolution: The First Generation of Americans* (Cambridge, MA: Harvard University Press, 2000). On the limits of this transformation, see "Forum: How Revolutionary Was the Revolution? A Discussion of Gordon Wood's *The Radicalism of the American Revolution*," *William and Mary Quarterly* 51 (1994), 679–716.

[11]The larger economic transformation has often been described as the "market revolution." For an overview of this period, see Charles Sellers, *The Market Revolution: Jacksonian America, 1815–1846* (New York: Oxford University Press, 1991).

[12]Barnum, *Life of P. T. Barnum* (1855), 30–35; Saxon, *P. T. Barnum*, 29–30.

[13]Barnum, *Life of P. T. Barnum* (1855), 218–219.

[14]Fanny Trollope, *Domestic Manners of the Americans* (London: Whitaker, Treacher, and Company, 1832), 2:137–138. A similar assessment appears in William O'Bryan, *A Narrative of Travels in the United States of America* (London: Gilbert and Company, 1836), 406–407.

[15]P. T. Barnum, *Humbugs of the World; An Account of Humbugs, Delusions, Impositions, Quackeries, Deceits, and Deceivers Generally, in All Ages* (New York: Carleton, 1866), 16–17.

[16]Constance Rourke, *Trumpets of Jubilee* (New York: Harcourt Brace, 1927), 406–414; Harris, *Humbug*, 75; *The Knickerbocker; Or, New York Monthly Magazine*, January 1855, 45.

[17]*Knickerbocker*, 45. For a sense of the contents of the museum, see *Barnum's American Museum Illustrated* (New York: William Van Norden and Frank Leslie, 1850). On the American Museum generally, see Andrea Stulman Dennett, *Weird and Wonderful: The Dime Museum in America* (New York: NYU Press, 1997), 23–37.

[18]Saxon, *P. T. Barnum*, 108; Bruce A. McConachie, "Museum Theatre and the Problem of Respectability for Mid-Century Urban Americans," in Ron Engle and Tice L. Miller, *The American Stage: Social and Economic Issues from the Colonial Period to the Present* (Cambridge, UK: Cambridge University Press, 1993), 65–80; Adams, *E Pluribus Barnum*, 90–97.

[19]*New York Atlas*, February 16, 1845, quoted in Saxon, *P. T. Barnum*, 83. Helpful discussions of Barnum's complicated views on race can be found in both Adams, *E Pluribus Barnum*, and Eric Lott, *Love and Theft: Blackface Minstrelsy and the American Working Class* (New York: Oxford University Press, 1993), 79–81.

[20]The best account of the Joice Heth affair is Benjamin Reiss, *The Showman and the Slave: Race, Death, and Memory in Barnum's America* (Cambridge, MA: Harvard University Press, 2001).

[21]*New-York Daily Tribune*, November 15, 1853, 7. On Barnum and this particular play, see John Frink, *Uncle Tom's Cabin on the American Stage and Screen* (New York: Palgrave MacMillan, 2012), 71–106. On the "What Is It?" exhibition, see James W. Cook, *The Arts of Deception: Playing with Fraud in the Age of Barnum* (Cambridge, MA: Harvard University Press, 2001), 119–162.

[22]Saxon, *P. T. Barnum*, 82–85, 139, 205.

[23]Saxon, *P. T. Barnum*, 215–218. On New York City during this period, see Edward K. Spann, *Gotham at War: New York City, 1860–1865* (Wilmington, DE: Scholarly Resources, 2002).

[24]Saxon, *P. T. Barnum*, 222–223.

[25]P. T. Barnum, *Funny Stories Told by Phineas T. Barnum* (New York and London: Routledge, 1890), 294. Of course, Barnum followed up this compliment with a series of racist jokes, once again walking the fine line between multiple constituencies.

[26]"Literary Items," *United States Magazine*, March 15, 1855, 1.

[27]Harris, *Humbug*, 5. On the central place of failure in the nineteenth-century American economy, see Scott Sandage, *Born Losers: A History of Failure in America* (Cambridge, MA: Harvard University Press, 2005).

[28]Freedley's book went on to become a bestseller of its own, going through multiple editions. Edwin Troxell Freedley, *A Practice Treatise on Business* (Philadelphia: Lippincott, Grambo & Company, 1853), 306–312.

[29]Barnum, *Life of P. T. Barnum* (1855), 109. On Barnum and temperance, see Steven Belleto, "Drink versus Printer's Ink: Temperance and the Management of Financial Speculation in *The Life of P. T. Barnum*," *American Studies* 46 (2005), 45–65.

[30]"Iranistan, the Villa of P. T. Barnum, Esq., Bridgeport," *Litchfield Republican*, November 14, 1850, 1. On Iranistan, Barnum, and the architect behind the house, see Kathryn E. Holliday, *Leopold Eidlitz: Architecture and Idealism in the Gilded Age* (New York: W. W. Norton & Company, 2008), 90–91.

[31]Barnum's bankruptcy, as Arthur Saxon has noted, could easily fill a separate book. For a brief account, see Saxon, *P. T. Barnum*, 184–205. For Jerome's side of the story, see Chauncey Jerome, *A History of the American Clock Business for the Past Sixty Years* (New Haven, CT: F. C. Dayton, 1860), 106–114.

[32]*Plattsburgh Republican*, February 9, 1856, 3; "Barnum (the Showman) a Bankrupt," *The Observer* (London), April 14, 1856, quoting the *New York Herald*, unknown date.

[33]"Sympathy for Barnum," *New-York Daily Tribune*, April 25, 1856, 5; Saxon, *P. T. Barnum*, 184–205.

[34]Barnum, *The Life of P. T. Barnum* (1888), 168–191; Paul J. Boxell, "P. T. Barnum's Lecture for Londoners," *Quarterly Journal of Speech* 54 (1968), 140–146; Saxon, *P. T. Barnum*, 201–202.

[35]P. T. Barnum, *Struggles and Triumphs: Or, Forty Years' Recollections of P. T. Barnum, Written by Himself* (London: Sampson, Low, Son, and Marston, 1869).

[36]Barnum, *Life of P. T. Barnum* (1888), 314.

[37]John Kuo Wei Tchen, *New York before Chinatown: Orientalism and the Shaping of American Culture, 1776–1882* (Baltimore, MD: Johns Hopkins University Press, 2001),

117–148; Adams, *E Pluribus Barnum*, 164–192; David Weir, *American Orient: Imagining the East from the Colonial Era to the Present* (Amherst: University of Massachusetts Press, 2011), 176–179.

[38]Philip B. Kunhardt Jr., Philip B. Kunhardt III, and Peter W. Kunhardt, *P. T. Barnum: America's Greatest Showman* (New York: Knopf, 1995), 114–115; Susan J. Pearson, "'Infantile Specimens': Showing Babies in Nineteenth-Century America," *Journal of Social History* 42 (2008), 341–370; Blain Roberts, *Pageants, Parlors, and Pretty Women: Race and Beauty in the Twentieth-Century South* (Chapel Hill: University of North Carolina Press, 2014), 111–112.

[39]Barnum, *Life of P. T. Barnum* (1888), 61.

[40]Barnum, *Life of P. T. Barnum* (1888), 185–186. On Barnum and the history of advertising, see especially Jackson Lears, *Fables of Abundance: A Cultural History of Advertising in America* (New York: Basic Books, 1995), 51–63, 213–215, 226–227.

[41]Freedley, *A Practical Treatise on Business*, 199.

[42]Eric D. Lehman, *Becoming Tom Thumb: Charles Stratton, P. T. Barnum, and the Dawn of American Celebrity* (Middletown, CT: Wesleyan University Press, 2013); David Haven Blake, *Walt Whitman and the Culture of American Celebrity* (New Haven, CT: Yale University Press), 41, 48–49.

[43]Barnum, *Life of P. T. Barnum* (1855), 296–343; Frances Cavanah, "Jenny Lind Fever," *Historic Preservation* (1970), 15–24; W. Porter Ware and Thaddeus C. Lockard Jr., *P. T. Barnum Presents Jenny Lind: The American Tour of the Swedish Nightingale* (Baton Rouge: Louisiana State University Press, 1980).

[44]Barnum, *Life of P. T. Barnum* (1888), 343. In characteristic fashion, Barnum embroidered this anecdote in a later publication, making Grant's reply even more dramatic. See P. T. Barnum, *Funny Stories*, 361. On the story of the letter, see "Mr. Barnum, America," *New York Times*, March 1, 1885, 4.

PART TWO

Life of P. T. Barnum
Written by Himself

I. MY EARLY HISTORY

My first appearance upon this stage was on the 5th day of July, Anno Domini 1810. Independence Day had gone by, the cannons had ceased to thunder forth their remembrances of our Nation's Anniversary, the smoke had all cleared away, the drums had finished their rattle, and when peace and quiet were restored, I made my *début*. . . .

I am not aware that my advent created any peculiar commotion in the village, though my good mother declares that I made a great deal of noise the first hour I saw the light, and that she has never been able to discover any cessation since.

I must pass by the first seven years of my life—during which my grandfather crammed me with sugar and loaded me with pennies, to buy raisins and candies, which he always instructed me to solicit from the store-keeper at the "lowest cash price"—and proceed to talk of later events.

I commenced going to school at the age of about six years. The first date which I recollect inscribing upon my writing-book, was 1818. A school-house in those days was a thing to be dreaded—a schoolmaster, a kind of being to make the children tremble. My first school-teacher was a Mr. Camp, the second Mr. Zerah Judson, the third a Mr. Curtiss from Newtown, the fourth Dr. Orris T. Taylor, and afterwards my uncle Alanson Taylor, etc. In the summers Miss Hannah

Starr, an excellent teacher, of whom I was an especial favorite, and for whom I have ever entertained the highest respect, was our school-mistress. The first three male teachers used the ferule[1] prodigiously, and a dark dungeon which was built in the house, was tenanted nearly all the time during school hours, by some unlucky juvenile frequently under eight years of age, who had incurred the displeasure of the "one-man power."

I was generally accounted a pretty apt scholar, and as I increased in years, there were but two or three in school who were considered my superiors. In arithmetic I was unusually quick, and I recollect, at the age of twelve years, being called out of bed one night by my teacher, who had laid a small wager with a neighbor that I could figure up and give the correct number of feet in a load of wood in five minutes. The neighbor stated the dimensions, and as I had no slate in the house I marked them on the stove pipe, and thereon also figured my calculations, and gave the result in less than two minutes, to the great delight of my teacher, my mother, and myself, and to the no small astonishment of our incredulous neighbor. My father was a tailor, a farmer, and sometimes a tavernkeeper; so I was often kept out of school, and never had any "advantages" except at the common district school, and one summer at the "Academy" in Danbury, a distance of three miles, which I marched and countermarched six times per week.

Like most farmers' boys, I was obliged to drive and fetch the cows, carry in firewood, shell corn, weed beets and cabbages, and, as I grew larger, I rode horse for ploughing, turned and raked hay, and in due time handled "the shovel and the hoe," as well as the plough; but I never really liked to work. . . .

My organ of acquisitiveness[2] must be large, or else my parents commenced its cultivation at an early period. Before I was five years of age I began to accumulate pennies and sixpennies. At the age of six years my grandfather informed me that all my little pieces of coin amounted to one dollar, and if I would go with him and take my money, he would show me something worth having. Placing all my wealth in a pocket handkerchief which was closely wound up and firmly grasped, I started with my grandfather. He took me to the village tavern, then kept by Mr. Stiles Wakelee, and approaching the landlord, he said, "Here, Mr. Wakelee, is

[1]A flat piece of wood used by teachers to discipline children.

[2]In the mid-nineteenth century, a pseudoscience known as phrenology became popular. It held that a person's character could be divined by the shape of their head, with particular areas of the skull, or "organs," connected to different personality traits.

the richest boy in this part of the country. He has a dollar in cash. I wish you to take his change and give him a silver dollar for it."

The complaisant landlord took my deposits and presently handed me a silver dollar.

Never have I seen the time (nor shall I ever again) when I felt so rich, so absolutely independent of all the world, as I did when I looked at that monstrous big silver dollar, and felt that it was all my own. Talk of "cart wheels," there was never one half so large as that dollar looked to me. I believed, without the slightest reservation, that this entire earth and all its contents could be purchased by that wonderful piece of bullion, and that it would be a bad bargain at that.

But my dollar did not long remain alone. My mother taught me that I should still save my pennies, and I did so. As I grew larger, my grandfather paid me ten cents per day for riding the horse which preceded the ox-team in ploughing, and I hit upon various expedients for adding to my pile. On "training days," instead of spending money, I was earning it in the vocation of a peddler. My stock in trade consisted of a gallon of molasses, boiled down and worked into molasses candy, called in those times "cookania," and I usually found myself a dollar richer at the end of "training," than I was at the commencement. As I always had a remarkable taste for speculation, my holiday stock soon increased, and comprised "ginger-bread," cookies, sugar candies, and cherry rum. The latter article consisted of a demijohn of New-England rum, in which was put a quantity of wild cherries, and I believe a little sugar. I soon learned that the soldiers were good cherry-rum customers, and no sooner did I hear the words "halt," "ground arms," than I approached the "trainers" with my decanter and wine-glass. In a few years I should have been a second Crœsus in wealth, had not my father considerately allowed me to purchase my own clothing. This arrangement kept my pile reduced to a moderate size. Always looking out for the main chance, however, I had sheep of my own, a calf of which I was the sole proprietor, and other individual property which made me feel, at twelve years of age, that I was quite a man of substance.

I felt at the same time that I had not reached my proper sphere. The farm was no place for me. I always disliked work. Headwork I was excessively fond of. I was always ready to concoct fun, or lay plans for money-making, but hand-work was decidedly not in my line. My father insisted that I could hoe and plough and dig in the garden as well as anybody else, but I generally contrived to shirk the work altogether, or by slighting it, get through with the day's work. . . .

II. CLERK IN A STORE—ANECDOTES

My aversion to hand-work, on the farm or otherwise, continued to be manifested in various ways, all of which was generally set down to the score of laziness. I believe, indeed, I had the reputation of being the laziest boy in town, probably because I was always busy at head-work to evade the sentence of gaining bread by the sweat of the brow. In sheer despair of making any thing better of me, my father concluded to try me as a merchant. He had previously erected a suitable building in Bethel, and taking Mr. Hiram Weed as a partner, they purchased a stock of dry goods, groceries, hardware, and a thousand other "notions;" and I was duly installed as clerk in a country store.

Like many greenhorns[3] before me, this was the height of my ambition. I felt that it was a great condescension on my part to enter into conversation with the common boys who had to work for a living. I strutted behind the counter with a pen back of my ear, was wonderfully polite to ladies, assumed a wise look when entering charges upon the day-book, was astonishingly active in waiting upon customers, whether in weighing tenpenny nails, starch, indigo, or saleratus[4], or drawing New-England rum or West India molasses.

Ours was a cash, credit and barter store; and I drove many a sharp trade with old women who paid for their purchases in butter, eggs, bees-wax, feathers, and rags, and with men who exchanged for our commodities, hats, axe-helves, oats, corn, buck-wheat, hickory-nuts, and other commodities. It was something of a drawback upon my dignity that I was compelled to sweep the store, take down the window-shutters, and make the fire; nevertheless the thought of being a "merchant" fully compensated me for all such menial duties.

My propensities for money-making continued active as ever, and I asked and obtained the privilege of purchasing candies on my own account, to sell to the juvenile portion of our customers. I received a small salary for my services, (my father as usual stipulating that I should clothe myself,) and I intended to be faithful to my employers; but I have found, all through life, that wherever there are conflicting interests, men are very apt to think of self first, and so I fear it was with me,—for I well remember spending much time in urging indulgent mothers to buy candies for their darling children, when other customers were waiting to be served with more substantial articles of merchandise.

[3]An inexperienced person; a novice.
[4]Baking soda.

A country store in the evening, or upon a wet day, is a miserably dull place, so far as trade is concerned. Upon such occasions therefore I had little to do, and I will explain why the time did not hang unpleasantly upon my hands.

In nearly every New-England village, at the time of which I write, there could be found from six to twenty social, jolly, storytelling, joke-playing wags and wits, regular originals, who would get together at the tavern or store, and spend their evenings and stormy afternoons in relating anecdotes, describing their various adventures, playing off practical jokes upon each other, and engaging in every project out of which a little fun could be extracted by village wits whose ideas were usually sharpened at brief intervals by a "treat," otherwise known as a glass of Santa Cruz rum, old Holland gin, or Jamaica spirits.

Bethel was not an exception to this state of things. In fact no place of its size could boast more original geniuses in the way of joking and story-telling than my native village. . . . My grandfather, Phineas Taylor, was one of the sort. His near neighbor, Benjamin Hoyt, or "Esquire Hoyt," as he was called, on account of being a justice of the peace, was one of the most inveterate story-tellers I ever knew. He could relate an anecdote with better effect than any man I have ever seen. He would generally profess to know all the parties in the story which he related, and however comic it might be, he would preserve the most rigid seriousness of countenance until its *dénouement*, when he would break forth into a hearty haw! haw! which of itself would throw his hearers into convulsions of laughter.

Luckily or unluckily, our store was the resort of all these wits, and many is the day and evening that I have hung with delight upon their stories, and many the night that I have kept the store open until eleven o'clock, in order to listen to the last anecdotes of the two jokers who had remained long after their companions had gone to rest.

Inheriting a vital love of fun and an aptness for practical jokes, all that was said and done by these village wags was not only watched with the most intense pleasure by myself, but was also noted upon the tablets of a most retentive memory, whence I can now extract them without losing scarcely a word. Some of these specimens I will present to the reader hereafter. I will however here advert to a circumstance which will show how the whole neighborhood, as it were, would join in practising and perpetuating a joke.

It will be remembered that my grandfather, a few days after my birth, in consideration of my taking his name, presented me with a tract of land called "Ivy Island." I was not four years of age before my grandfather informed me, with much seriousness, that I was a landowner; that he had given me a valuable farm on account of my name, etc.; and I am certain that not a week elapsed, from that period till I was twelve years of age, that I did not hear of this precious patrimony. My grandfather never spoke of me in my presence, either to a neighbor or stranger, without saying that I was the richest child in town, because I owned all "Ivy Island," the most valuable farm in Connecticut. My mother often reminded me of my immense possessions, and my father occasionally asked me if I would not support the family when I came in possession of my property. I frequently assured my father, in the most perfect good faith, that he need give himself no uneasiness upon that score, for I would see that all the family wants were bountifully supplied when I attained my majority and received my estate. Our neighbors, too, reminded me a dozen times a day, that they feared I would refuse to play with their children, because I had inherited such immense wealth, while they had nothing of the sort.

These continual allusions to "Ivy Island," for six or eight years, I fear excited my pride, and I know that the prospect made me wish that the slow-moving wheels of time would attain a rapidity which would hurry up that twenty-first birth-day, and thus enable me to become the nabob,[5] which my grandfather's generous foresight had cut me out for. How often, too, did I promise my playmates, when they rendered me a kind action, that when I became of age they should have a slice of "Ivy Island" that would make them rich for life! I sincerely intended to fulfil these promises to the letter. But, alas for the mutability of human affairs! an issue was at hand which I little expected, and one which was destined to effect a serious change in my hopes and aspirations.

One summer (I think it was 1822, at which period I was twelve years old) I asked my father's permission to visit "Ivy Island." He promised I should do so in a few days, as we should be getting hay in that vicinity. I scarcely slept for three nights, so great was my joy to think that, like Moses of old, I should be permitted to look upon the promised land. The visions of wealth which had so long haunted me in relation to that valuable locality now became intensified, and I not only felt that it must be a land flowing with milk and honey, but caverns of emeralds, diamonds, and other precious stones, as well as mines of silver and gold, opened vividly to my mind's eye.

[5]Someone of great wealth and status.

The wished-for morning at length arrived, and my father informed me that we were to mow in the meadow adjoining "Ivy Island," and that I might visit it with our hired man during "nooning." My grandfather kindly reminded me that when I came to look upon the precious spot, I was to remember that I was indebted to his bounty, and that if I had not been named "Phineas" I never could have been the proprietor of "Ivy Island." My mother, too, had to put in a word.

"Now, Taylor," said she, "don't become so excited when you see your property as to let your joy make you sick, for remember, rich as you are, that it will be nine years before you can come into possession of your fortune." I promised to be calm and reasonable.

"If you visit Ivy Island," she continued, "you will lose your rest at noon, and you will feel tired, after turning hay all the forenoon. Had you not better lie under the trees and rest at 'nooning,' and visit Ivy Island at some other time?"

"No, my dear mother," I replied," I don't care for nooning, I shall not feel tired, and I am so anxious to step upon my property; that I cannot wait any longer."

"Well, go," said my mother; "but don't feel above speaking to your brothers and sisters when you return."

I felt that this injunction was not altogether superfluous, for I already began to feel that it was rather degrading for me to labor as hard as those who had no estate settled upon them.

We went to work in our meadow. It was situated in that part of "Plum-Trees" known as "East Swamp." When we arrived at the meadow I asked my father where "Ivy Island" was.

"Yonder, at the north end of this meadow, where you see those beautiful trees rising, in the distance," he replied.

I looked towards the place indicated, and my bosom swelled with inexpressible pride and delight, as I beheld for the first time the munificent gift of my honored and generous grandsire.

The forenoon soon slipped away; I turned the grass as fast as two men could cut it, and after making a hasty repast with my father and the workmen under the shade trees, our favorite "hired man," a good-natured Irishman named Edmund, taking an axe upon his shoulders, told me he was ready to go with me to visit "Ivy Island."

I started upon my feet with delight, but could not restrain asking him why he took an axe. He replied that perhaps I would like to have him cut into some of the beautiful specimens of timber upon my property, in order that I could see how superior it was in quality to that found in any other part of the world. His answer was perfectly satisfactory, and we started. As we approached the north end of the meadow the ground became swampy and wet, and we found great difficulty in proceeding. We were obliged to leap from bog to bog, and frequently making a mis-step, I found myself up to my middle in water. . . .

Half a dozen hornets now attacked me, and I involuntarily ducked my head under the water. When I popped out again my tormenters had disappeared, and I waded on as well as I could towards "Ivy Island." After about fifteen minutes, during which time I floundered through the morass, now stepping on a piece of submerged wood, and anon slipping into a hole, I rolled out upon dry land, covered with mud, out of breath, and looking considerably more like a drowned rat than a human being.

"Thank the Merciful Powers, ye are safe at last," said my Irish companion.

"Oh, what a dreadful time I have had, and how that hornet's sting smarts!" I groaned, in misery.

"Niver mind, my boy; we have only to cross this little creek, and ye'll be upon yer own valuable property," was the encouraging reply.

I looked, and behold we had arrived upon the margin of a stream ten or twelve feet wide, the banks of which were so thickly lined with alders that a person could scarcely squeeze between them.

"Good heavens!" I exclaimed, "is my property surrounded with water?"

"How the divil could it be 'Ivy *Island*' if it was not?'" was the quick response.

"Oh! I had never thought about the meaning of the name," I replied; "but how in the world can we get across this brook?"

"Faith, and now you'll see the use of the axe, I am thinking," replied Edmund, as he cut his way through the alders, and proceeded to fell a small oak tree which stood upon the bank of the stream. This tree fell directly across the brook, and thus formed a temporary bridge, over which Edmund kindly assisted me.

I now found myself upon "Ivy Island," and began to look about me with curiosity.

"Why, there seems to be nothing here but stunted ivies and a few straggling trees!" I exclaimed.

"How else could it be 'Ivy Island?'" was the quiet answer.

I proceeded a few rods towards the centre of my domain, perfectly chop-fallen. The truth rushed upon me. I had been made a fool of by all our neighborhood for more than half a dozen years. My rich "Ivy

Island" was an inaccessible piece of barren land, not worth a farthing, and all my visions of future wealth and greatness vanished into thin air. While I stood pondering upon my sudden downfall, I discovered a monstrous black snake approaching me, with upraised head and piercing black eyes. I gave one halloo and took to my heels. The Irishman helped me across the temporary bridge, and this was my first and *last* visit to "Ivy Island!" We got back to the meadow, and found my father and men mowing away lustily.

"Well, how do you like your property?" asked my father, with the most imperturbable gravity.

"I would sell it pretty cheap," I responded, holding down my head.

A tremendous roar of laughter bursting from all the workmen showed that they were in the secret. On returning home at night, my grandfather called to congratulate me, with as serious a countenance as if "Ivy Island" was indeed a valuable domain, instead of a barren waste, over which he and the whole neighborhood had chuckled ever since I was born. My mother, too, with a grave physiognomy, hoped I had found it as rich as I anticipated. Several of our neighbors called to ask if I was not glad now, that I was named Phineas; and from that time during the next five years I was continually reminded of the valuable property known as "Ivy Island."

I can the more heartily laugh at this practical joke, because that inheritance was long afterwards of service to me. "Ivy Island" was a part of the weight that made the wheel of fortune begin to turn in my favor at a time when my head was downward. . . .

V. A BATCH OF INCIDENTS

. . . My father was brought to his bed with a severe attack of fever in March, and departed this life, I trust for a better world, on the 7th of September, 1825, aged 48 years.

I was then fifteen years of age. I stood by his bedside. The world looked dark indeed, when I realized that I was for ever deprived of my paternal protector! I felt that I was a poor inexperienced boy, thrown out on the wide world to shift for myself, and a sense of forlornness completely overcame me. My mother was left with five children. I was the oldest, and the youngest was only seven years of age. We followed the remains of husband and parent to their resting-place, and returned to our desolate home, feeling that we were forsaken by the world, and that but little hope existed for us this side the grave.

Administrators to the estate were appointed, and the fact was soon apparent that my father had not succeeded in providing any of this world's goods for the support of his family. The estate was declared *insolvent*, and it did not pay fifty cents upon a dollar. My mother, like many widows before her, was driven to many straits to support her little family, but being industrious, economical and persevering, she succeeded in a few years in redeeming the homestead and becoming its sole possessor. The few dollars which I had accumulated, I had loaned to my father, and held his note therefor, but it was decided that the property of a minor belonged to the father, and my claim was ruled out. I was subsequently compelled to earn as clerk in a store the money to pay for the pair of shoes that were purchased for me to wear at my father's funeral. I can truly say, therefore, that I began the world with nothing, and was barefooted at that.

I remained with Mr. Weed as clerk but a little longer, and then removed to "Grassy Plain," a mile north-west of the village of Bethel, where I engaged with James S. Keeler and Lewis Whitlock, as clerk in their store, at six dollars per month and my board—my mother doing my washing. I soon entered into speculations on my own account, and by dint of economy succeeded in getting a little sum of money ahead. I boarded with Mrs. Jerusha Wheeler and her daughters, Jerusha and Mary. As nearly everybody had a nick-name, the two former ladies were called "Rushia"—the old lady being designated "Aunt Rushia." They were an exceedingly nice and worthy family, and made me an excellent home. I chose my uncle Alanson Taylor as my "guardian," and was guided by his counsel. I was extremely active as a clerk, was considered a 'cute trader, and soon gained the confidence and esteem of my employers. I remember with gratitude that they allowed me many facilities for earning money.

On one occasion a peddler called at our store with a large wagon filled with common green glass bottles of various sizes, holding from half a pint to a gallon. My employers were both absent, and I bantered him to trade his whole load of bottles in exchange for goods. Thinking me a greenhorn, he accepted my proposition, and I managed to pay him off in unsaleable goods at exorbitant prices. Soon after he departed, Mr. Keeler returned and found his little store half filled with bottles!

"What under heavens have you been doing?" said he in surprise.

"I have been trading goods for bottles," said I.

"You have made a fool of yourself," he exclaimed, "for you have bottles enough to supply the whole town for twenty years."

I begged him not to be alarmed, and promised to get rid of the entire lot within three months.

"If you can do that," said he, "you can perform a miracle."

I then showed him the list of goods which I had exchanged for the bottles, with the extra prices annexed, and he found upon figuring that I had bartered a lot of worthless trash at a rate which brought the new merchandise to considerably less than one-half the wholesale price. He was pleased with the result, but wondered what could be done with the bottles. We stowed away the largest portion of them in the loft of our store.

My employers kept what was called a *barter* store. Many of the hat manufacturers traded there and paid us in hats, giving "store orders" to their numerous employees, including journeymen,[6] apprentices, female hat trimmers, etc., etc. Of course we had a large number of customers, and I knew them all intimately.

I may say that when I made the bottle trade I had a project in my head for selling them all, as well as getting rid of a large quantity of tinware which had been in the store for some years, and had become begrimed with dirt and fly-specks. That project was a *lottery.* On the first wet day, therefore, when there were but few customers, I spent several hours in making up my scheme. The highest prize was $25, payable in any kind of goods the customer desired. Then I had fifty prizes of $5 each, designating in my scheme what goods each prize should consist of. For instance, one $5 prize consisted of one pair cotton hose, one cotton handkerchief, two tin cups, four pint glass bottles, three tin skimmers, one quart glass bottle, six tin nutmeg graters, eleven half-pint glass bottles, etc., etc. — the glass and tinware always forming the greater portion of each prize. I had one hundred prizes of one dollar each, one hundred prizes of fifty cents each, and three hundred prizes of twenty-five cents each. There were one thousand tickets at fifty cents each. The prizes amounted to the same as the tickets — $500. I had taken an idea from the church lottery, in which my grandfather was manager, and had many prizes of only half the cost of the tickets. I headed the scheme with glaring capitals, written in my best hand, setting forth that it was a "MAGNIFICENT LOTTERY!" "$25 FOR ONLY 50 CTS.!!" "OVER 550 PRIZES!!!" "ONLY 1000 TICKETS!!!!" "GOODS PUT IN AT THE LOWEST CASH PRICES!!!!!" etc., etc., etc.

---

[6] A craftsman who had completed a period of training as an apprentice, but who had not yet set up shop as a master artisan.

The tickets went like wildfire. Customers did not stop to consider the nature of the prizes. Journeymen hatters, boss hatters, apprentice boys, and hat trimming girls bought tickets. In ten days they were all sold. A day was fixed for the drawing of the lottery, and it came off punctually, as announced.

The next day, and for several days thereafter, adventurers came for their prizes. A young lady who had drawn five dollars would find herself entitled to a piece of tape, a spool of cotton, a paper of pins, sixteen tin skimmers, cups, and nutmeg graters, and a few dozen glass bottles of various sizes! She would beg me to retain the glass and tinware and pay her in some other goods, but was informed that such a proceeding would be contrary to the rules of the establishment and could not be entertained for a moment.

One man would find all his prizes to consist of tinware. Another would discover that out of twenty tickets, he had drawn perhaps ten prizes, and that they consisted entirely of glass bottles. Some of the customers were vexed, but most of them laughed at the joke. The basket loads, the arms full, and the bags full of soiled tin and glass bottles which were carried out of our store during the first few days after the lottery drawing, constituted a series of most ludicrous scenes. Scarcely a customer was permitted to depart without one or more specimens of tin or green glass. Within ten days every glass bottle had disappeared, and the old tinware was replaced by a smaller quantity as bright as silver. . . .

My grandfather enjoyed my lottery speculation very much, and seemed to agree with many others, who declared that I was indeed "a chip of the old block." . . .

On Saturday nights I usually went to Bethel to remain with my mother and attend church on the Sabbath. My mother continued for some years to keep the village tavern. One Saturday evening a violent thunder shower came up; it was very dark, and rained in torrents, with occasional intervals of a few minutes. Miss Mary Wheeler (who was a milliner[7]) sent word across to the store that there was a girl at her house from Bethel, who had come up on horseback to obtain her new bonnet, that she was afraid to return home alone, and if I was going to Bethel on horseback that night, she wished me to escort her customer. I assented, and in a few minutes my horse was at "Aunt Rushia's" door. I went in, and was introduced to a fair, rosy-cheeked, buxom-looking girl, with beautiful white teeth, named "Chairy Hallett."

---

[7]A maker of hats and head ware.

Of course "Chairy" was a nickname, which I subsequently learned meant "Charity."

I assisted the young lady into her saddle, was soon mounted on my own horse, and we trotted slowly towards Bethel.

The brief view that I had of this girl by candle-light, had sent all sorts of agreeable sensations through my bosom. I was in a state of feeling quite new to me, and as unaccountable as it was novel. I opened a conversation with her, and finding her affable and in no degree prim or "stuck-up," (although she was on horseback,) I regretted that the distance to Bethel was not five miles instead of one. A vivid flash of lightning at that moment lighted up the horizon, and gave me a fair view of the face of my interesting companion. I then wished the distance was twenty miles at the least. I was not long in learning that she was a tailoress, working with Mr. Zerah Benedict, of Bethel. The tailoring trade stood much higher in my estimation from that moment than it ever did before. We soon arrived at Bethel, and bidding my fair companion good night, I went to my mother's. That girl's face haunted me in my dreams that night. I saw her the next day at church, and on every subsequent Sunday for some time, but no opportunity offered that season for me to renew the acquaintance.

Messrs. Keeler and Whitlock sold out their store of goods to Mr. Lewis Taylor in the summer of 1827. I remained a short time as clerk for Mr. Taylor. They have a proverb in Connecticut, that "the best school in which to have a boy learn human nature, is to permit him to be a tin peddler for a few years." I think his chances for getting "his eye-teeth cut" would be equally great, in a country barter store like that in which I was clerk. As before stated, many of our customers were hatters, and we took hats in payment for goods. The large manufacturers generally dealt pretty fairly by us, but some of the smaller fry occasionally shaved us prodigiously. There probably is no trade in which there can be more cheating than in hats. If a hat was damaged "in coloring" or otherwise, perhaps by a cut of half a foot in length, it was sure to be patched up, smoothed over, and slipped in with others to send to the store. Among the furs used for the nap of hats in those days, were beaver, Russia, nutria, otter, coney,[8] muskrat, etc., etc. The best fur was otter, the poorest was coney.

The hatters mixed their inferior furs with a little of their best, and sold us the hats for "otter." We in return mixed our sugars, teas, and liquors,

---

[8]Rabbit.

and gave them the most valuable names. It was "dog eat dog"—"tit for tat." Our cottons were sold for wool, our wool and cotton for silk and linen; in fact nearly every thing was different from what it was represented. The customers cheated us in their fabrics: we cheated the customers with our goods. Each party expected to be cheated, if it was possible. Our eyes, and not our ears, had to be our masters. We must believe little that we saw, and less that we heard. Our calicoes were all "fast colors," according to our representations, and the colors would generally run "fast" enough and show them a tub of soap-suds. Our ground coffee was as good as burned peas, beans, and corn could make, and our ginger was tolerable, considering the price of corn meal. The "tricks of trade" were numerous. If a "peddler" wanted to trade with us for a box of beaver hats worth sixty dollars per dozen, he was sure to obtain a box of "coneys" which were dear at fifteen dollars per dozen. If we took our pay in clocks, warranted to keep good time, the chances were that they were no better than a chest of drawers for that purpose—that they were like Pindar's razors,[9] made to sell," and if half the number of wheels necessary to form a clock could be found within the case, it was as lucky as extraordinary.

Such a school would "cut eye-teeth," but if it did not cut conscience, morals, and integrity all up by the roots, it would be because the scholars quit before their education was completed! . . .

VI. INCIDENTS AND VARIOUS SCHEMES

In the autumn of 1826 Mr. Oliver Taylor, who had removed from Danbury to Brooklyn, Long Island, a few years previously, offered me the position of clerk in his grocery store. He had also a large comb factory in Brooklyn and a comb store in New-York. I accepted Mr. Taylor's offer. The store was at the corner of Sands and Pearl streets. . . .

I had not been long in Mr. Taylor's employment before I became conversant with the routine of the business, and the purchasing of all the goods for the store was soon intrusted to me. I bought for cash entirely, and thus was enabled to exercise my judgment in making purchases—sometimes going into all sections of the lower part of the city in search of the cheapest markets for groceries. I also frequently

[9]Peter Pindar was the pseudonym of English satirist and poet John Wolcot; his poem "The Razor Seller" described how a peddler unloaded worthless goods on a credulous customer.

attended the wholesale auctions of teas, sugars, molasses, etc., so that by watching the sales, noting the prices, and recording the names of buyers, I knew what profits they were realizing, and how far I could probably beat them down for cash. At these auctions I occasionally made the acquaintance of several grocers who wanted small lots of the goods offered for sale, and we frequently clubbed together and bid off a lot which, being divided between us, gave each about the quantity he desired, and at a reduced price from what we should have been compelled to pay if the goods had passed into other hands and thus been taxed with another profit.

My employer manifested great interest in me, and treated me with the utmost kindness, but the situation did not suit me. The fact is, there are some persons so constituted that they can never be satisfied to labor for a fixed salary, let it be never so great. I am one of that sort. My disposition is, and ever was, of a speculative character, and I am never content to engage in any business unless it is of such a nature that my profits may be greatly enhanced by an increase of energy, perseverance, attention to business, tact, etc. As therefore I had no opportunity to speculate on my own account in this Brooklyn store, I soon became uneasy. Young as I was, (and probably because I was so young,) I began to think seriously of going into business for myself, and although I had no capital to start on, several men of means had offered to furnish the money and join me in business. I was just then at an uneasy age—in a transition state—neither boy nor man—an age when it is of the highest importance that a youth should have some discreet friend and instructor on whose good counsel he can rely. How self-conceited, generally, are boys from sixteen to eighteen years old. They feel that they are fully competent to transact business which persons much older than they, know requires many years' experience. This is the age, too, when the "eighteen-year-old fever" is apt to make fools of young men in other than a business point of view. Boys of this age, and girls of twelve to sixteen, are undoubtedly the most disagreeable persons in the world. They are so wild, so stubborn and self-sufficient, that reflecting parents have great reason for deep anxiety as to the "turn" which they may take. . . .

In February, 1828, my grandfather wrote me that if I would come to Bethel and establish some kind of business for myself, he would allow me to occupy, rent free, one half of his carriage-house. I had a strong desire to return to my native village, and after several weeks' reflection I accepted his offer.

The carriage-house referred to was situated on the public street in Bethel, and I concluded to finish off one part of it, and open a retail fruit and confectionery store. Before leaving New-York, I consulted several fruit dealers with whom I was acquainted, and made arrangements for sending them my orders. I then went to Bethel, arranged the building, put in a small stock of goods, including a barrel of ale, and opened my establishment on the first Monday morning in May, 1828, that being our military training day.

The hopes and fears which agitated me for weeks previously to this my first grand opening, have probably never had a parallel in all my subsequent adventures. I was worth about one hundred and twenty dollars, and I invested all I possessed in this enterprise. It cost me fifty dollars to fit up my little store, and seventy dollars more purchased my stock in trade. I am suspicious that I received little good from attending church the day previously to opening my store, for I distinctly remember being greatly exercised in mind for fear it would rain the next day, and thus diminish the number of customers for my cakes, candies, nuts, raisins, etc.

I was up betimes on Monday morning, and was delighted to find the weather propitious. The country people began to flock into the village at an early hour, and the novelty of my little shop, which was set out in as good style as I was capable of, attracted their attention. I soon had plenty to do, and before noon was obliged to call in one of my old school-mates to assist me in waiting upon my numerous customers. Business continued brisk during the whole day and evening, and when I closed I had the satisfaction of counting out sixty-three dollars as my day's receipts! My entire barrel of ale was sold, but the assortment of other goods was not broken up, nor apparently very seriously diminished, so that although I had received the entire cost of my goods, less seven dollars, the stock on hand showed that my profits had been excellent.

I need not attempt to relate how gratified I was by the result of my first day's experiment. I considered my little store as a "fixed fact," and such it proved to be. I put in another barrel of ale, and proceeding to New-York, expended all of my money for a small stock of fancy goods, and such articles as I thought would find a ready sale. My assortment included pocket-books, combs, beads, cheap finger-rings, pocket-knives, and a few toys. My business continued good during the summer, and in the fall I added stewed oysters to my assortment.

My grandfather had great pleasure in my success, and advised me to take the agency of some lottery dealer for the sale of lottery tickets on commission. Lotteries were at that time legal in Connecticut, and were generally considered as legitimate a branch of business as any other. I therefore adopted my grandfather's advice, and obtained an agency for selling lottery tickets on a commission of ten per cent. This business, connected with the fruit, confectionery, oyster, and toy establishment, rendered my profits quite satisfactory. . . .

About this time I made arrangements to go to Pittsburgh, Pa., with Mr. Samuel Sherwood, of Bridgeport, on an exploring expedition. I had heard that there was a fine opening in that city for a lottery office, and Sherwood and myself concluded to try our fortunes there, provided we found the prospects equal to our anticipations. We called at the office of the New-York managers, Yates & McIntyre, and had an interview with their chief business man, Mr. Dudley S. Gregory—at present ex-mayor and a large proprietor in Jersey City. . . .

Our visit to the New-York lottery managers greatly enlightened me in regard to the profits of that line of business. I had been in the habit of selling tickets for Washington Yale, the editor and printer in Danbury, also for O. W. Sherwood and his cousin Samuel of Bridgeport, for a commission of 10 to 15 per cent; but in my interviews with Mr. Gregory, I learned that the managers, taking to themselves the fifteen per cent deducted on all prizes, furnished tickets to their agents at what was called "scheme price," which allowed the agents from 25 to 30 per cent profit. The lotteries being drawn by combination numbers, the public generally had no knowledge whatever of the number of tickets in a lottery; the managers, therefore, made the prizes amount to less than the retail price of tickets by 25 or 30 per cent. This extra percentage was a shave[10] additional to the 15 per cent allowed in old-fashioned lotteries. . . .

After learning the *profitable* basis of the foregoing facts, I went to our Connecticut lottery managers, and from that time obtained my tickets directly from them at "the scheme price." In my turn I established agents all through the country, and my profits were immense. I sold from five hundred to two thousand dollars' worth of tickets per day. About this time my uncle Alanson Taylor joined me as a partner in the lottery business, and proved a very efficient salesman. . . .

Selling so many tickets as I did, a prize of one or two thousand dollars, and numerous smaller ones, must occasionally turn up. These, being duly trumpeted, rendered mine the "lucky office" in the estimation of

---

[10]A cut of the profits.

many. I received orders from distant parts of the country by mail, and
sent out tickets on commission by post-riders and others. Among my
"private customers" were a number of clergymen and deacons; and
occasionally some of the weak brothers of the "Shakers,"[11] who came to
Bethel to sell garden seeds, bought a few lottery tickets "on the sly." . . .

I still kept a close eye upon the attractive tailoress, Charity Hallett;
and although my good mother and some other relatives feared that
I was not looking high enough in the world, those who knew the girl
best declared that she was an industrious, excellent, sensible, and well-
behaved girl, and some of them added that "she was altogether too
good for Taylor Barnum." I perfectly agreed with them in their conclusions, and in the summer of 1829 I proved it by asking her hand in
marriage. My suit was accepted, and the wedding day appointed. In the
mean time I applied myself closely to business, no person suspecting
that the "event" was near at hand. In October my "sweetheart" went to
New-York, ostensibly to visit her uncle, Nathan Beers, who resided at
No. 3 Allen street. I left home on Saturday, November 7, for New-York,
having particular occasion to purchase goods for our little store. On the
next evening, by the aid of the Rev. Dr. McAuley, and in the presence
of sundry relatives and friends of hers, the tailoress changed her name
to Mrs. Charity Barnum, and I became the husband of one of the best
women that was ever created.

I was at that time little more than nineteen years of age. I have long
felt assured, that had I waited twenty years longer, I could not have found
another woman so well suited to my disposition, and so valuable as a
wife, a mother, and a friend; yet I do not approve of nor recommend too
early marriages. Young persons' minds should become more matured
before they venture to decide upon the most important event which
can occur to them in a lifetime. Marriage has been called "a lottery,"
"taking a leap in the dark," etc. It is, to say the least, a serious ordinance,
deserving serious thought. Hasty marriage, and especially the marriage
of boys and girls, has, in my opinion, been the cause of untold misery
in thousands of instances, the advice of that worthy old philosopher,
Ben Franklin, to the contrary notwithstanding.

The bride and bridegroom returned to Bethel the same week, and
took board in the family where she had previously resided. My mother
received me as if nothing had happened, and made no allusion to the
wedding. She evidently felt chagrined at the clandestine manner of my

[11]A religious sect that flourished at this time; its members took vows of chastity and
lived in tightly regulated farm communes.

marriage; but I called on her every day with the same freedom that I had ever done, and within a month she invited me to bring "my wife" and spend the following Sabbath with her. I did so; and from that day to this, I am sure that neither she nor any other person ever said or believed that I had not been extremely fortunate in the selection of my companion. . . .

VII. STRUGGLING—JOICE HETH—VIVALLA

In the winter of 1834–35, I removed my family to New-York, having hired a house in Hudson street. Strictly speaking, I entered that great city to "seek my fortune." Lotteries in the State of Connecticut had been prohibited by law; I had lost large amounts of money by my private customers, some of whom had gone beyond their means in purchasing tickets, while others had put their property out of their hands, and thus defrauded me of considerable sums. I was also a large loser by the mercantile business, and must confess, in addition, that the old proverb, "Easy come easy go," was too true in my case. I had learned that I could make money rapidly and in large sums, whenever I set about it with a will, and I did not hesitate to expend it in various extravagances as freely as I gained it. I acquired it so readily, that I did not realize the worth of it, and I entertained no anxiety whatever about laying it up. To be sure, I thought that at *some future time* I should begin to accumulate by saving, but I cared not for the present, and hence I scattered my means with an open and unsparing hand.

When I removed to New-York, I had no pecuniary resources except such as were derived from old debts left in the hands of an agent in Bethel for collection.

I had hoped to find an opening with some mercantile firm in New-York, where for my services I could receive a portion of the profits, for I had a disposition which ever revolted at laboring for a fixed salary. I wanted an opportunity where my faculties and energies could have full play, and where the amount of profits should depend entirely upon the amount of tact, perseverance and energy, which I contributed to the business. But I could not find the situation I coveted. My resources began to fail me, and, my family being in ill-health, I found it difficult to maintain them. In order to do so, I secured the situation of "drummer"[12] to several stores, including the cap and stock store of Mr. Chapman in Chatham street,

---

[12] A door-to-door salesman.

the proprietors of which allowed me a small commission on all sales which they made to customers whom I introduced.

This of course was only a temporary arrangement, and, like "Micawber,"[13] I was continually on the look-out for something better to "turn up." Every morning at sunrise my eyes were running over the columns of "Wants" in the New-York "Sun,"[14] hoping to hit upon something that would suit me. Many is the wild-goose chase which I had in pursuit of a situation so beautifully and temptingly set forth among those "wants." Fortunes equalling that of Crœsus, and as plenty as blackberries, were dangling from many an advertisement which mysteriously invited the reader to apply at Room No. 16, in the fifth story of a house in some retired and uninviting locality; but when I had wended my way up flights of dark, rickety, greasy stairs, and through sombre, narrow passages, I would find that my fortune depended firstly upon my advancing a certain sum of money, from three dollars to five hundred as the case might be; and secondly, upon my success in peddling a newly discovered patent life-pill, an ingenious mouse-trap, or something of the sort. . . .

In the latter part of July, 1835, Mr. Coley Bartram, of Reading, Ct., and at present a resident of the same State, called at our store. He informed us that he had owned an interest in an extraordinary negro woman, named Joice Heth, whom he believed to be one hundred and sixty-one years of age, and whom he also believed to have been the nurse of General Washington. He had sold out his interest to his partner R. W. Lindsay, of Jefferson County, Kentucky, who was now exhibiting her in Philadelphia, but not having much tact as a showman, he was anxious to sell out and return home.

Mr. Bartram also handed me a copy of "The Pennsylvania Inquirer," of July 15, 1835, and directed my attention to the following advertisement, which I here transcribe *verbatim*:

Curiosity—The citizens of Philadelphia and its vicinity have an opportunity of witnessing at the Masonic Hall, one of the greatest natural curiosities ever witnessed, viz., JOICE HETH, a negress aged 161 years, who formerly belonged to the father of Gen.

---

[13]A character in Charles Dickens's *David Copperfield*. Micawber, a bankrupt, remains optimistic that his luck will change and repeatedly utters the phrase: "something will turn up." He eventually attains financial security.

[14]The *Sun* was one of a handful of cheap newspapers known collectively as the "penny press" that made their debut in New York City in the 1830s.

Washington. She has been a member of the Baptist Church one hundred and sixteen years, and can rehearse many hymns, and sing them according to former custom. She was born near the old Potomac River in Virginia, and has for ninety or one hundred years lived in Paris, Kentucky, with the Bowling family.

All who have seen this extraordinary woman are satisfied of the truth of the account of her age. The evidence of the Bowling family, which is respectable, is strong, but the original bill of sale of Augustine Washington, in his own handwriting, and other evidence which the proprietor has in his possession, will satisfy even the most incredulous.

A lady will attend at the hall during the afternoon and evening for the accommodation of those ladies who may call.

The New-York newspapers had already furnished descriptions of this wonderful personage, and becoming considerably excited upon the subject, I proceeded at once to Philadelphia and had an interview with Lindsay at the Masonic Hall.

I was favorably struck with the appearance of the old woman. So far as outward indications were concerned, she might almost as well have been called a thousand years old as any other age. She was lying upon a high lounge in the middle of the room; her lower extremities were drawn up, with her knees elevated some two feet above the top of the lounge. She was apparently in good health and spirits, but former disease or old age, or perhaps both combined, had rendered her unable to change her position; in fact, although she could move one of her arms at will, her lower limbs were fixed in their position, and could not be straightened. She was totally blind, and her eyes were so deeply sunken in their sockets that the eyeballs seemed to have disappeared altogether. She had no teeth, but possessed a head of thick bushy gray hair. Her left arm lay across her breast, and she had no power to remove it. The fingers of her left hand were drawn down so as nearly to close it, and remained fixed and immovable. The nails upon that hand were about four inches in length, and extended above her wrist. The nails upon her large toes also had grown to the thickness of nearly a quarter of an inch.

She was very sociable, and would talk almost incessantly so long as visitors would converse with her. She sang a variety of ancient hymns, and was very garrulous when speaking of her protégé "dear little George," as she termed the great father of our country. She declared that she was present at his birth, that she was formerly the slave of Augustine Washington, the father of George, and that she was the first person who put clothes upon him. "In fact," said Joice, and it was a favorite expression of hers, "I raised him." She related many interesting anecdotes of "her dear little George," and this, mixed with her conversations upon religious subjects, for she claimed to be a member of the Baptist Church, rendered her exhibition an extremely interesting one.

I asked Mr. Lindsay for the proofs of her extraordinary age, and he exhibited what purported to be a bill of sale ‑from Augustine Washington, of the county of Westmoreland, Virginia, to "Elizabeth Atwood," of "one negro woman, named Joice Heth, aged fifty-four years, for and in consideration of the sum of thirty-three pounds lawful money of Virginia." The document bore the date "fifth day of February, one thousand seven hundred and twenty-seven," and was "sealed and delivered in presence of Richard Buckner and William Washington."

The story told by Lindsay and "Aunt Joice" was, that Mrs. Elizabeth Atwood was a sister-in-law of Augustine Washington, that the husband of Joice was a slave of Mrs. Atwood, and for that reason the above sale was made. As Mrs. Atwood was a near neighbor of Mr. Washington, Aunt Joice was present at the birth of "little George," and she having long been the old family nurse, was the first person called upon to clothe the new-born infant.

The story seemed plausible, and the "bill of sale" had every appearance of antiquity. It was exhibited in a glass frame, was very sallow in appearance, and seemed to have been folded for such a great length of time that the folds were worn nearly through, and in some parts entirely so.

I inquired why the existence of such an extraordinary old woman had not been discovered and made known long ago. The reply was that she had been lying in an out-house of John S. Bowling of Kentucky for many years, that no one knew or seemed to care how old she was, that she had been brought thither from Virginia a long time ago, and that the fact of her extreme age had been but recently brought to light by the discovery of this old bill of sale in the Record office in Virginia, by the son of Mr. Bowling, who, while looking over the ancient papers in that office, happened to notice the paper endorsed Joice Heth, that his curiosity was excited, and from inquiries made in that neighborhood he was convinced that the document applied to his father's old slave then living, and who was therefore really one hundred and sixty-one years of age; that he thereupon took the paper home, and became confirmed in regard to the identity of Joice with the slave described in that paper.

This whole account appeared to me satisfactory, and I inquired the price of the negress. Three thousand dollars was the sum named, but before leaving Philadelphia I received from Mr. Lindsay a writing, stipulating that I should have the right at any time within ten days to become her owner upon paying to him the sum of one thousand dollars.

With this paper I started for New-York, determined if possible to purchase Joice Heth. I did not possess more than five hundred dollars in cash, but my glowing representations to a friend, of the golden harvest which I was sure the exhibition must produce, induced him to loan me the other five hundred dollars, and . . . I returned to Philadelphia with the money, and became the proprietor of the negress. . . .

I applied to Mr. William Niblo,[15] who, I believe, had seen the old negrees in Philadelphia. He did not recognize me as the person who a few months previously had applied to him for the situation of bar-keeper. We soon made a bargain for the exhibition of Aunt Joice in one of the large apartments in his dwelling-house in the vicinity of his saloon, which was at that time a large, open and airy establishment where musical and light entertainments were given, the guests during the intermission, as well as at other times, being supplied with ice-creams and other refreshments, in little alcove-boxes fitted up with tables, and running nearly all the distance around his garden.

These alcoves were tastefully decorated on the outside with festoons of lamps of variegated colors, and the grand walk through the middle of the garden was illuminated on each side by chaste and pretty transparencies, about seven feet high and two feet wide, each surmounted with a large globular lamp. These transparencies were then new in the city of New-York, and were very attractive. They were gotten up by W. J. and H. Hannington, who have since become so celebrated for glass-staining and decorative painting. Mr. H. Hannington prepared me several transparencies, two feet by three in size, which I had placed upon a hollow frame and lighted from the inside. It was painted in colors with white letters, and read — Joice Heth 161 Years Old.

The terms of my engagement with Mr. Niblo were these: He was to furnish the room and lights, pay the expense of printing, advertising, and a ticket-seller, and retain therefor one half of the gross receipts. The result proved an average of about $1500 per week.

I engaged as an assistant in exhibiting "Aunt Joice" Mr. Levi Lyman. He was a lawyer by profession, and had been practising in Penn Yan, N.Y. He was a shrewd, sociable, and somewhat indolent Yankee; possessed a good knowledge of human nature; was polite, agreeable, could converse on most subjects, and was admirably calculated to fill the position for which I engaged him.

---

[15]Niblo was the proprietor of the Grand Saloon, one of the premier entertainments venues in New York City.

Of course, in carrying out my new vocation of showman, I spared no reasonable efforts to make it successful. I was aware of the great power of the public press, and I used it to the extent of my ability. Lyman wrote a brief memoir of Joice, and putting it into a pamphlet form, illustrated with her portrait, sold it to visitors on his own account, at six cents per copy.

I had the same portrait printed on innumerable small bills, and also flooded the city with "posters," setting forth the peculiar attractions which "the nurse of Washington" presented. . . .

Our exhibition usually opened with a statement of the manner in which the age of Joice Heth was discovered, as well as the account of her antecedents in Virginia, and a reading of the bill of sale. We would then question her in relation to the birth and youth of General Washington, and she always gave satisfactory answers in every particular. Individuals among the audience would also frequently ask her questions, and put her to the severest cross-examinations, without ever finding her to deviate from what had every evidence of being a plain unvarnished statement of facts.

Joice was very fond of church-music, to which she would beat time by waving her long withered arm. On one occasion in New-York an aged Baptist minister stood by her side as she was singing one of her favorite hymns, and he joined her, and lined each verse. She was much pleased by this circumstance, and sang with renewed animation. After the hymn was finished, the clergyman lined off the verse of another hymn, and Joice immediately remarking, "I know that hymn," joined him in singing it. He lined in this manner several hymns which were entirely new to me, and in each case Joice knew them, and in one or two instances refreshed his memory when he found himself at a loss to recall the exact language of the verses. Joice loved to converse upon religious subjects, and frequently insisted on the attendance of clergymen for that purpose.

The question naturally arises, if Joice Heth was an impostor, *who* taught her these things? and how happened it that she was so familiar, not only with ancient psalmody, but also with the minute details of the Washington family? To all this, I unhesitatingly answer, *I do not know.* I taught her none of these things. She was perfectly familiar with them all before I ever saw her, and she taught me many facts in relation to the Washington family with which I was not before acquainted.

From Providence, where the exhibition was highly successful, we went to Boston. This was my first appearance in the modern Athens, and I saw much that was new and interesting to me. I attended various churches, and was pleased to see such an almost universal observance of the Sabbath. The theatres, too, were not permitted to be open on Saturday evenings, and my mind reverted to the customs of many of our neighbors in Connecticut, who, according to the old Puritan fashion, "kept Saturday night," that is, they considered that the Sabbath commenced with the setting of the sun on Saturday and closed at sundown on Sunday, at which time they would recommence their labors and recreations.

We opened our exhibition in the small ball-room of Concert Hall, at the corner of Court and Hanover streets. The fame of Joice had preceded her, the city was well posted with large bills announcing her coming, and the newspapers had heralded her anticipated arrival in such a multiplicity of styles, that the public curiosity was on tip-toe. I remember that one of the papers, after giving a description of Joice Heth, and the great satisfaction which her exhibition had given in New-York, added, "It *rejoice-heth* us exceedingly to know that we shall be permitted to look upon the old patriarch."

The celebrated Maelzel was exhibiting his equally celebrated "automaton chess-player" in the large ball-room of Concert Hall; but the crowd of visitors to see Aunt Joice was so great, that our room could not accommodate them, and Mr. Maelzel was induced to close his exhibition, and give us his large room. I had frequent interviews and long conversations with Mr. Maelzel. I looked upon him as the great father of caterers for public amusement, and was pleased with his assurance that I would certainly make a successful showman.

"I see," said he, in broken English, "that you understand the value of the press, and that is the great thing. Nothing helps the showmans like the types and the ink. When your old woman dies," he added, "you come to me, and I will make your fortune. I will let you have my 'carousal,' my automaton trumpet-player, and many curious things which will make plenty of money."

I thanked him for his generous proposals, and assured him that should circumstances render it feasible, I should apply to him.

Our exhibition room continued to attract large numbers of visitors for several weeks before there was any visible falling off. I kept up a constant succession of novel advertisements and unique notices in the newspapers, which tended to keep old Joice fresh in the minds of the public, and served to sharpen the curiosity of the people.

When the audiences began to decrease in numbers, a short communication appeared in one of the newspapers, signed "*A Visitor*," in which the writer claimed to have made an important discovery. He stated that

Joice Heth, as at present exhibited, was a humbug, whereas if the simple truth was told in regard to the exhibition, it was really vastly curious and interesting. "The fact is," said the communication, "Joice Heth is not a human being. What purports to be a remarkably old woman is simply a curiously constructed automaton, made up of whalebone, india-rubber, and numberless springs ingeniously put together, and made to move at the slightest touch, according to the will of the operator. The exhibitor is a ventriloquist, and all the conversations apparently held with the ancient lady are purely imaginary, so far as she is concerned, for the answers and incidents purporting to be given and related by her, are merely the ventriloquial voice of the exhibitor."

Maelzel's ingenious mechanism somewhat prepared the way for this announcement, and hundreds who had not visited Joice Heth were now anxious to see the curious automaton; while many who had seen her were equally desirous of a second look, in order to determine whether or not they had been deceived. The consequence was, our audiences again largely increased. . . .

From Boston we went to Hingham, and thence in succession to Lowell, Worcester, Springfield, and Hartford, meeting with most satisfactory success. Everywhere there appeared to be conviction of the extreme longevity of Joice.

We hastened our return to New-York to fill a second engagement I had made with Mr. Niblo. . . .

From Niblo's we went to New-Haven for three days, where the crowds were as large as usual. We then returned to New-York and proceeded to Newark, where I met with the usual success. From Newark we returned to New-York and went to Albany for one week to fill an engagement made with Mr. Meech, the proprietor of the Museum.

While exhibiting there, light evening entertainments were given in the theatre of the Museum, one part of which consisted of remarkable feats of balancing, plate spinning, stilt walking, etc., by "Signor Antonio." The balancing and spinning of crockery was nearly or quite new in this country—to me it was entirely so. It was also as surprising as it was novel. The daring feats of Antonio upon stilts, his balancing guns with the bayonets resting on his nose, and various other performances which I had never seen before, attracted my attention. I inquired of Mr. Meech where Antonio came from. He informed me that he was an Italian—had sailed from England to Canada, whence he had proceeded to Albany, and had never exhibited in any other American city. Learning that Mr. Meech did not desire his services after that week, I sought an interview with "Antonio," and in ten minutes engaged him to perform for me in any portion of the United States for one year from date, at the salary of $12 per week, besides board and travelling expenses. I did not know exactly where I should use my protégé, but I was certain that there was money in him, and thus I became interested in my second show.

Antonio, Joice Heth, Lyman and myself, left Albany for New-York, stopping at the private boarding house in Frankfort street which I had taken the spring previous, but had sold out soon after engaging Aunt Joice. I left my two shows in Frankfort street while I went to join my wife and daughter, who were boarding with a Mr. Knapp, in Cherry street.

The first favor which I asked of Antonio was, that he should submit to be thoroughly washed — an operation to which he had apparently been a stranger for several years; and the second, that he should change his name. I did not think "Antonio" sufficiently "foreign," hence I named him Signor Vivalla, to both which propositions he consented. I immediately wrote a notice announcing the extraordinary qualities of Signor Vivalla, who had just arrived from Italy, elaborately setting forth the wonders of his performances. This was published as an article of news in one of the city papers, and I forwarded a dozen copies to the several theatrical managers in New-York, and elsewhere.

I first called upon William Dinneford, Esq., manager of the Franklin Theatre, but he declined engaging the "eminent Italian artist." He had seen so many performances of that kind which were vastly more extraordinary than any thing which Vivalla could do, he would not think of engaging him.

"Now," says I, "Mr. Dinneford, I beg your pardon, but I must be permitted to say that you are mistaken. You have no doubt seen strange things in your life, but, my dear sir, I should never have imported Signor Vivalla from Italy, unless I had authentic evidence that he was the only artist of the kind who ever left that country."

"What are your terms?" asked Dinneford, who (like many worthy young ladies, and many other republicans of the first water) was evidently beginning to melt under the magic influence of a foreign importation.

"You shall have him one night for nothing," I replied. "If you like him after one trial, you shall have him the remainder of the week for fifty dollars — but, understand me, this is only that the public may be able to see what he is. After that, my terms are $50 per night."

My proposition for the one night was accepted. I invoked the powers of "printer's ink" and wood-cuts for three days and nights previous to the first appearance of "the renowned and extraordinary Italian artist, Signor Vivalla," and they were potent for my purpose. The house was crammed. I marched upon the stage as a supernumerary to assist Vivalla in arranging his plates and other "crockery ware," to hand him the gun to fire when he had divested himself of one of his stilts, and was hopping across the stage on one stilt ten feet high, and to aid him in handling his muskets, etc.

The applause which followed each of the Italian's feats was tremendous. It was such as only a Chatham or a Bowery audience could give. Manager Dinneford was delighted, and before we left the stage he engaged Vivalla for the week. At the termination of the performances Vivalla was called before the curtain, and as I did not consider it policy for him to be able to speak English, (although he could do so very well, having travelled several years in England,) I went out with him and addressed the audience in his name, thanking them for their generosity, and announcing him for the remainder of the week. . . .

Vivalla and myself proceeded to Philadelphia, and opened at the Walnut street, on the 26th, to a slim house. . . .

"Signor Vivalla's" performances were well received. On the second night, however, I heard two or three distinct hisses from the pit. It was the first time that my protégé had received the slightest mark of disapprobation since I had engaged him, and I was surprised. Vivalla, who, under my management, had become proud of his profession, was excessively annoyed. I proceeded, therefore, to that portion of the house whence the hissing emanated, and found that it came from a circus performer named Roberts and his friends. It seems that Roberts was a balancer and juggler, and he declared he could do all that Vivalla could. I was certain he could *not*, and told him so. Some hard words ensued. I then proceeded to the ticket-office, where I wrote several copies of a "card," and proceeding to the printing-offices of various news papers, climbing up narrow stairs and threading dark alleys for the purpose, I secured its appearance in the papers of the next morning. The card was headed "*One Thousand Dollars Reward!*" and then proceeded to state that Signor Vivalla would pay the foregoing sum to any man who would publicly accomplish his (Vivalla's) feats, at such public place as Vivalla should designate.

Roberts came out with a card the next day, acccepting Vivalla's offer, calling on him to put up the thousand dollars, to name the time and place of trial, and stating that he could be found at a certain hotel near Green's Circus, of which he was a member. I borrowed a thousand dollars of my friend Oliver Taylor—went to Mr. Warren, treasurer of the Walnut, and asked him what share of the house he would give me if I would get up an excitement that should bring in four or five hundred dollars a night. (The entire receipts the night previous were but seventy-five dollars.) He replied that he would give me one third of the gross receipts. I told him I had a crotchet in my head, and would inform him within an hour whether it would work. I then called upon Roberts and showed him my thousand dollars. "Now," says I, "I am ready to put up this money in responsible hands, to be forfeited and paid to you if you accomplish Signor Vivalla's feats."

"Very well," said Roberts, with considerable bravado; "put the money into the hands of Mr. Green, the proprietor of the circus"—to which I assented.

"Now," said I, "I wish you to sign this card, to be published in handbills and in to-morrow's newspapers." He read it. It stated that Signor Vivalla having placed one thousand dollars in hands satisfactory to himself, to be forfeited to him if he succeeded in performing the various feats of the said Vivalla, he (Roberts) would make the public trial to do so on the stage of the Walnut street Theatre, on the night of the 30th inst.

"You don't expect me to perform *all* of Vivalla's feats, do you?" said Roberts, after reading the card.

"No, I don't *expect* you *can*, but if you do *not*, of course you will not win the thousand dollars," I replied.

"Why, I know nothing about walking on stilts, and am not fool enough to risk my neck in that way," said Roberts.

Several persons, circus-riders and others, had crowded around us, and exhibited some degree of excitement. My thousand dollars was still openly displayed in my hand. I saw that Roberts was determined to back out, and as that would not be consistent with my plans, I remarked that he and I could do our own business without the intermeddling of third parties, and I would like to see him alone. . . .

The next day I brought Roberts and Vivalla privately together, and by practising they soon discovered what tricks each could accomplish, and we then proceeded to arrange the manner in which the trial should come off, and how it should terminate.

In the mean time the excitement about the coming trial of skill was fast increasing. Suitable "notices" were inserted in the papers, bragging that Roberts was an American, and could beat the foreigner all hollow. Roberts in the mean time announced in the papers that if, as he expected, he should obtain the thousand dollars, a portion of it should be disbursed for charitable purposes. I set "The Press" at work lustily, in the shape of handbills, squibs, etc. Before the night of trial arrived, the excitement had reached fever heat. I knew that a crowded house was *un fait accompli*.

I was not disappointed. The pit and upper boxes were crowded to suffocation. In fact, the sales of tickets to these localities were stopped because no more persons could possibly gain admittance. The dress circle was not so full, though even that contained many more persons than had been in it at one time during the previous two or three months.

The contest was a very interesting one. Roberts of course was to be beaten, and it was agreed that Vivalla should at first perform his *easiest* feats, in order that the battle should be kept up as long as possible. Roberts successively performed the same feats that Vivalla did. Each party was continually cheered by his friends and hissed by his opponents. Occasionally some of Roberts's friends from the pit would call out, "Roberts, beat the little French man," "One Yankee is too much for two Frenchmen any time," etc. The contest lasted about forty minutes, when Roberts came forward and acknowledged himself defeated. He was obliged to give up on the feat of spinning two plates at once, one in each hand. His friends urged him to try again, but on his declining, they requested him to perform his own peculiar feats, (juggling, tossing the balls, etc.). This he did, and his performances, which continued for twenty minutes, were highly applauded.

As soon as the curtain fell, the two contestants were called for. Before they went out I had concluded a private arrangement with Roberts for a month—he to perform solely as I directed. When he went before the curtain, therefore, he informed the audience that he had a lame wrist, which was indeed the fact. He further informed them that he could do more feats of various kinds than Vivalla could, and he would challenge Vivalla to such a trial at any time and place he pleased, for a wager of five hundred dollars.

"I accept that challenge," said Vivalla, who stood at Roberts's side, "and I name next Tuesday night in this theatre."

"Bravo," cried Vivalla's friends, as vigorously as "bravo" had been shouted by the friends of Roberts.

Three hearty cheers were given by the enthusiastic audience, and the antagonists, looking daggers at each other, withdrew at opposite sides of the curtain. Before the uproar of applause had ceased, Roberts and Vivalla had met upon the stage, shaken hands, and were enjoying a hearty laugh. . . .

The receipts of the theatre on that night were $593.25, of which I received one third—$197.75. . . .

These details may possess little interest to the general reader. They however serve to show (though it may be revealing some of the "tricks of the trade") how such matters are frequently managed in theatres and other places of amusement. The people are repeatedly wrought to excitement and take sides most enthusiastically in trials of skill, when, if the truth were known, the whole affair is a piece of management between the prominent parties. The entertainment of the time may be an offset to the "humbug" of the transaction, and it may be doubted whether managers of theatres will be losers by these revelations of mine, for the public appears disposed to be amused even when they are conscious of being deceived.

Meanwhile poor old Joice had sickened, and with her attendant, a faithful colored woman whom I hired in Boston, had gone to my brother's house in Bethel, where she was provided with warm apartments and the best medical and other assistance.

On the 21st of February, 1836, my brother's horses and sleigh stopped at the door of my boarding-house in New-York. The driver handed me a letter from my brother Philo, stating that Aunt Joice was no more. She died at his house on Friday night, the 19th, and her body was then in the sleigh, having been conveyed to New-York for me to dispose of as I thought proper. I at once determined to have it returned to Bethel and interred in our village burial-ground, though for the present it was placed in a small room of which I had the key.

The next morning I called on an eminent surgeon who, upon visiting Joice at Niblo's, had expressed a desire to institute a postmortem examination if she should die in this country. I agreed that he should have the opportunity, if unfortunately it should occur while she was under my protection. I now informed him that Aunt Joice was dead, and he reminded me of my promise. I admitted it, and immediately proceeded to arrange for the examination to take place on the following day.

In the mean time a mahogany coffin and plate were procured and taken to the hall where the examination was to take place. A large number of physicians, students, and several clergymen and editors were present. Among the last named class was Richard Adams Locke, author of the celebrated "Moon Hoax,"[16] who was at that time editor of the New-York Sun.

---

[16]In 1835, the editor of the *Sun*, a popular New York newspaper, published a series of articles purportedly written by a well-known British astronomer that reported telescopic observation of life on the moon. The articles vividly described unicorns, winged humans, bipedal beavers, and other creatures.

An absence of ossification of the arteries in the immediate region of the heart was deemed by the dissector and most of the gentlemen present an evidence against the assumed age of Joice.

When all had withdrawn excepting the surgeon, his particular friend Locke, Lyman, and myself, the surgeon remarked, addressing me, that there was surely some mistake in regard to the alleged age of Joice; that instead of being 161 years old, she was probably not over eighty.

I stated to him, in reply, what was strictly true, that I had hired Joice in perfect good faith, and relied upon her appearance and the documents as evidence of the truth of her story. The same gentleman had examined her when alive on exhibition at Niblo's. He rejoined that he had no doubt I had been deceived in the matter, that her personal appearance really did indicate extreme longevity, but that the documents must either have been forged, or else they applied to some other individual.

Lyman, who was always ready for a joke, no matter what the cost nor at whose expense, here made a remark regarding the inability of the faculty to decide with much precision in regard to a case of this kind. His observations wounded the feelings of the surgeon, and taking the arm of his friend Locke, they left the hall—I fear in not very good humor.

The "Sun" of the next day (Feb. 25, 1836) contained an editorial, written of course by Locke, commencing as follows:

"Dissection of Joice Heth—precious humbug exposed—The anatomical examination of the body of Joice Heth yesterday, resulted in the exposure of one of the most precious humbugs that ever was imposed upon a credulous community."

Mr. Locke then proceeded to give a scientific account of the dissection, and the reasons he had for doubting her story. . . .

Locke's editorial asserted that the age of Joice did not exceed seventy-five or eighty years.

When the "Sun" newspaper appeared, and the account of the post-mortem examination was read, thousands of persons who had seen her when alive, were much astonished. "There must be a mistake," said one, "for her very appearance indicated her age to have been at least a hundred and twenty." "She could not have been less than a hundred," said others; while still others believed she was quite as old as represented.

In this state of the public mind, Lyman determined to put a joke upon James Gordon Bennett, of the Herald.[17] He therefore called at Bennett's office and told him . . . that in fact Joice Heth was now being exhibited in

---

[17]The *Herald* was another popular newspaper in New York City and the *Sun*'s competitor.

Connecticut, and that the body which had been dissected as hers, was that of an old negress who had recently died at Harlem. Bennett swallowed the bait, hook and all. He declared it was the best hoax he ever heard of, eclipsing Locke's "moon hoax" entirely, and he proceeded to jot down the details as they were invented by Lyman's fertile brain. The result was, the appearance of the article from the Sun in the Herald of Feb, 27, 1836, preceded by the following remarks:

> "Another Hoax — Annexed is a long rigmarole account of the dissection of Joice Heth, extracted from yesterday's Sun, which is nothing more nor less than a complete hoax from beginning to end. *Joice Heth is not dead.* On Wednesday last, as we learn from the best authority, she was living at Hebron, in Connecticut, where she then was. The subject on which Doctor Rogers and the Medical Faculty of Barclay street have been exercising their knife and their ingenuity, is the remains of a respectable old negress called Aunt Nelly, who has lived many years in a small house by herself, in Harlem, belonging to Mr. Clarke. She is, as Dr. Rogers sagely discovers, and Doctor Locke his colleague accurately records, only eighty years of age. Aunt Nelly before her death complained of old age and infirmity. She was otherwise in good spirits. The recent winter, however, has been very severe, and so she gave up the ghost a few days ago.

. . . This editorial preface of the Herald introduced the account of the dissection as it appeared in the Sun; and Bennett subjoined the comprehensive comment: "Thus far the Joice Heth hoax, for the veracity of which we have names and certificates in our possession."

Upon reading the article from the Herald, a large portion of the public believed it, and consoled themselves by saying, "Ah, I was sure the old woman was considerably more than eighty. The article in the Herald makes the matter all clear."

Locke insisted that he had not been humbugged, and Bennett persisted that he had, and offered to lay a wager of several hundred dollars that Joice was really alive and then being exhibited in Connecticut! After a while the editor of the Herald, finding himself hoaxed, cried still the louder that he was right, and published several fictitious certificates purporting to have been written and signed by persons residing in Harlem, corroborating Lyman's story of "poor Aunt Nelly."

In September of the same year, (while I was absent at the South), Bennett met Lyman in the street, and proceeded to "blow him sky high" for having imposed upon him. Lyman laughed; he said he only meant it as a harmless joke, and that "now, as a recompense for the imposition, he would furnish Bennett with 'the veritable history of the rise, progress, and termination of the Joice Heth humbug.'"

Bennett was delighted. They went to his office, and Lyman dictated while the editor took down the heads of what purported to be the history of Joice—of her having been first found by me in the out-house of a plantation in Kentucky—of my having extracted all her teeth—taught her the Washington story—called her 110 years old in Louisville, 121 in Cincinnati—twenty years older in Pittsburgh, and 161 at Philadelphia.

This ridiculous story, being a ten times greater humbug than the one before practised upon the editor of the Herald, was duly written out and embellished by Bennett. . . .

The story of Lyman has since been generally accredited as the true history of the old negress, and never, until the present writing, have I said or written a word by way of contradiction or correction. Newspaper and social controversy on the subject (and seldom have vastly more important matters been so largely discussed) served my purpose as "a showman" by keeping my name before the public.

I will only add, that the remains of Joice were removed to Bethel, and buried respectably.

IX. THE AMERICAN MUSEUM

April 26, 1841, I called on Robert Sears, the publisher of "Sears' Pictorial Illustrations of the Bible," and contracted for five hundred copies of the work for $500, accepted the United States agency, opened an office, May 10, at the corner of Beekman and Nassau streets, which was subsequently taken by Mr. Redfield as a bookstore, and is the present site of the Nassau Bank. I had thus made another effort to quit the life of a showman for ever, and settle down into a respectable calling. I advertised largely, appointed agents and sub-agents, and managed in the course of six months to sell thousands of books, and at the same time to place a sufficient number in the hands of irresponsible agents to use up all my profits and all my capital! . . .

Living in the city of New-York with nothing to do and a family to support, in a very short time exhausted my funds, and I became about as poor as I should ever wish to be. I looked around in vain for employment congenial to my feelings, that would serve to keep my head above water. I finally obtained the post of writing advertisements and notices for the

Bowery Amphitheatre, my duties including daily visits to the upper stories of many newspaper offices to deliver what I had prepared, and see that they were inserted. For this I received $4.00 per week! and was thankful for even that.

I also wrote articles for the Sunday press, for the purpose of enabling me to "keep the pot boiling" at home.

These productions afforded me a fair remuneration, but it was at best a precarious way of living, and I began to realize, seriously, that I was at the very bottom round of fortune's ladder, and that I had now arrived at an age when it was necessary to make one grand effort to raise myself above want, and to think soberly of laying up something for "a rainy day." I had hitherto been careless upon that point. I had engaged in divers enterprises, caring little what the result was, so that I made a present living for my family. I now saw that it was time to provide for the future.

About this period, I received a letter from my esteemed friend, Hon. Thomas T. Whittlesey, of Danbury. He had long held a mortgage of $500 on a piece of property which I owned in that town. He wrote to say that he was satisfied I never would lay up any thing until I could "invent a riddle that would hold water," and as that was not very likely to occur, I might as well pay him now as ever. That letter strengthened the resolutions I had made, and laying it aside unanswered, I said to myself, "Now, Mr. B., no more nonsense, no more living from hand to mouth, but from this moment please to concentrate your energies upon providing permanently for *the future*."

While engaged as outside clerk for the Bowery Amphitheatre, I casually learned that the collection of curiosities comprising Scudder's American Museum,[18] at the corner of Broadway and Ann street, was for sale. It belonged to the daughters of Mr. Scudder, and was conducted for their benefit by John Furzman, under the authority of Mr. John Heath, administrator. The price asked for the entire collection was $15,000. It had cost its founder, Mr. Scudder, probably $50,000, and from the profits of the establishment he had been able to leave a large competency to his children. The Museum, however, had been for several years a losing concern, and the heirs were anxious to sell it.

It will not be considered surprising, under all the circumstances, that my speculative spirit should look in that direction for a permanent

---

[18]A popular museum founded in the 1790s. It contained a hodgepodge of stuffed animals, bones, wax figures, a two-headed lamb, historical artifacts, and other objects of interest.

investment. My recent enterprises had not indeed been productive, and my funds were decidedly low; but my family was in poor health, I desired to enjoy the blessing of a fixed home—and so I repeatedly visited that Museum as a thoughtful looker-on. I saw, or believed I saw, that only energy, tact and liberality were needed, to give it life and to put it on a profitable footing; and although it might have appeared presumptuous, on my part, to dream of buying so valuable a property without having any money to do it with, I seriously determined to make the purchase, if possible.

I met a friend one day in the street, and told him my intentions. *"You* buy the American Museum?" said he with surprise, for he knew that my funds were at ebb-tide; "what do you intend buying it with?"

"Brass," I replied, "for silver and gold I have none."

It was even so.

The Museum building, I learned, belonged to Mr. Francis W. Olmsted, a retired merchant, who had a suite of rooms in Park Place. How to approach this great man was a question. I was acquainted with no one who knew him, and to enter his presence without an introduction, I considered equivalent to being kicked out of his house. I therefore wrote him a letter, informing him that I desired to purchase the Museum collection, and that although I had no ready means, if it could be purchased upon a reasonable credit I was entirely confident that my tact and experience, added to a most determined devotion to business, would enable me to make the payments when due. On this basis I asked him to purchase the collection in his own name—give me a writing securing it to me provided I made the payments punctually, including the rent of his building—allow me twelve dollars and a half a week on which to support my family—and if at any time I failed to meet the instalment due, I would vacate the premises and forfeit all that might have been paid to that date. "In fact, Mr. Olmsted," I continued in my earnestness, "you may bind me in any way, and as tightly as you please—only give me a chance to dig out, or scratch out, and I will either do so or forfeit all the labor and trouble which I may have incurred."

I also endeavored to show Mr. Olmsted, that by making this arrangement he would secure a permanent tenant, whereas if I did not make the purchase the Museum would probably soon be closed. I added, that if he would have the goodness to grant me an interview, I should be happy to give him satisfactory references, and would also submit to any reasonable conditions which he might propose.

I took the letter myself, handed it to his servant, and in two days afterwards I received a reply, naming an hour for me to call on him.

I was there at the exact moment, and Mr. Olmsted expressed himself pleased with my punctuality. He eyed me closely, and put several home questions regarding my habits and antecedents. I told him frankly my experience in the way of caterer for public amusements—mentioned Vauxhall Garden, the circus, and several exhibitions that I had managed in the South.[19] I was favorably impressed with Mr. Olmsted's appearance and manner. He indeed tried to assume an austere look, and to affect the aristocrat; but I thought I could see the good, open-hearted, noble *man* peering through his eyes, and a subsequent intimate acquaintance proved the correctness of my impressions respecting him.

"Who are your references?" he inquired.

"Any man in my line," I replied; "from Edmund Simpson, manager of the Park Theatre or William Niblo, to Messrs. Welch, June, Titus, Turner, Angevine, or other circus or menagerie proprietors; also Moses Y. Beach of the New-York Sun."

"Can you get any of them to call on me?" he continued.

I informed him that I could, and it was arranged that they should call on him the next day, and myself the day afterwards. My friend Niblo willingly rode down in his carriage, and had an interview with Mr. Olmsted. Mr. Beach and several others among the gentlemen named also called, and on the following morning I waited upon the arbiter of my fate.

"I don't like your references, Mr. Barnum," said Mr. Olmsted abruptly, as soon as I entered the room.

I was confused, and said "I regretted to hear it."

"They all speak too well of you," he added, laughing; "in fact they talk as if they were all partners of yours, and intended to share the profits."

This intelligence, of course, pleased me. Mr. Olmsted then inquired if I could not induce some friend to give bonds as security that I should meet the instalments as they became due. I thought it was doubtful.

"Can you offer me any security in case I should make the purchase for you?" was his still more direct question.

I thought of several small pieces of land which I owned in Connecticut, but they were severely afflicted with mortgages. "I have some land and buildings in Connecticut, but there are encumbrances on them," I replied.

"Yes, yes; I don't want mortgaged property," said Mr. O.; "I should probably have to redeem it."

---

[19]After his success with Joice Heth, Barnum had led a traveling circus on a tour of the southern states.

During further conversation, it was agreed that if he concluded to make the purchase for me, he should retain the property until it was all paid for; and should also appoint (at my expense) a ticket-receiver and accountant, who should render him a weekly statement. It was further stipulated that I should take in an apartment in the adjoining building, hitherto used as a billiard-room, and allow therefor five hundred dollars per year, making the entire rent three thousand dollars per annum, on a lease of ten years. I felt that in all this I had been liberal in my propositions and agreements, and hoped that the wealthy landlord would demand no more concessions. But he wanted something more.

"Now," said he, " if you only had a piece of unencumbered real estate that you could offer as additional security, I think I might venture to negotiate with you."

This seemed the turning-point of my fortune. Thinks I to myself, "It is now or never," and memory rapidly ran over my small possessions in search of the coveted bit of land. *Ivy Island*, in all the beauty in which my youthful imagination had pictured it, came dancing to my relief. I hesitated an instant. He is amply secured already—so I thought within myself—and without *some* piece of land, I may lose the Museum altogether. I saw no particular harm in it, and after a moment's hesitation I replied:

"I have five acres of land in Connecticut which is free from all lien or encumbrance."

"Indeed! what did you pay for it?"

"It was a present from my late grandfather, Phineas Taylor, given me on account of my name."

"Was he rich?" inquired Mr. Olmsted.

"He was considered well off in those parts," I answered.

"Very kind in him to give you the land. It is doubtless valuable. But I suppose you would not like to part with it, considering it was a present."

"I shall not have to part with it, if I make my payments punctually," I replied, "and I am sure I shall do that."

"Well," said Mr. Olmsted, "I think I will make the purchase for you. At all events, I'll think it over, and in the mean time you must see the administrator and heirs of the estate—get their best terms, and meet me here on my return to town a week hence."

I withdrew, and proceeded at once to the house of Mr. John Heath, the administrator. His price was $15,000. I offered him $10,000, payable in seven equal annual instalments, with good security. He could not think of selling at that price, and I agreed to call again.

During the week I had several interviews with Mr. Heath, and it was finally agreed that I should have it for $12,000, payable as above—possession to be given on the 15th November. Mr. Olmsted assented to this, and a morning was appointed to draw and sign the writings. Mr. Heath appeared, but said he must decline proceeding any farther in my case, as he had sold the collection to the directors of Peale's Museum (an incorporated institution) for $15,000, and had received $1000 in advance.

I was thunderstruck. I appealed to his honor. He replied that he had signed no writing with me, was not therefore legally bound, and he felt it his duty to do the best he could for the orphan girls. Mr. Olmsted said he was sorry for me, but could not help me. He would now have permanent tenants who would not require him to incur any risk, and I must necessarily be thrown overboard.

I withdrew, with feelings which I need not attempt to describe. I immediately informed myself as to the character of this Peale's Museum Company.[20] It proved to consist of a company of speculators, headed by an unsuccessful ex-president of a bank, who had bought Peale's collection for a few thousand dollars, were now to join the American Museum with it, issue and sell stock to the amount of $50,000, pocket $30,000 profits, and permit the stock-holders to look out for themselves.

I went immediately to several of the editors, including Major M. M. Noah, M. Y. Beach, my good friends, West, Herrick and Ropes, of the Atlas, and others, and stated my grievances. "Now," said I, "if you will grant me the use of your columns, I'll blow that speculation sky-high." They all consented, and I wrote a large number of squibs, cautioning the public against buying the Museum stock, ridiculed the idea of a board of broken-down bank directors engaging in the exhibition of stuffed monkey and gander skins, appealed to the case of the Zoological Institute, which had failed by adopting such a plan as the one now proposed, and finally told the public that such a speculation would be infinitely more unwise than Dickens's "Grand United Metropolitan Hot Muffin[21] and Crumpet-baking and Punctual Delivery Company."

---

[20] A museum founded by the painter Charles Wilson Peale in 1784. Like Scudder's American Museum, this Philadelphia institution—which eventually had branches in New York and Baltimore—hosted an eclectic collection of animals, artwork, historical objects, and relics.

[21] A fictional startup company launched by unscrupulous promoters in Charles Dickens's novel *Nicholas Nickleby*, published in the 1830s.

The stock was as dead as a herring! I then went to Mr. Heath and solicited a confidential conversation. He granted it. I asked him when the directors were to pay the other $14,000. "On the 26th day of December, or forfeit the $1000 already paid," was the reply. I assured him that they would never pay it, that they could not raise it, and that he would ultimately find himself with the Museum collection on his hands, and if once I started off with an exhibition for the South, I would not touch the Museum at *any* price. "Now," said I, "if you will agree with me confidentially, that in case these gentlemen do not pay you on the 26th December, I may have it on the 27th for $12,000, I will run the risk, and wait in this city until that date." He readily agreed to the proposition, but said he was sure they would not forfeit their $1000.

"Very well," said I; "all I ask of you is, that this arrangement shall not be mentioned." He assented. "On the 27th day of December, at ten o'clock A. M., I wish you to meet me in Mr. Olmsted's apartments, prepared to sign the writings, provided this incorporated company do not pay you $14,000 on the 26th." He agreed to this, and by my request put it in writing.

From that moment I felt that the Museum was mine. I saw Mr. Olmsted, and told him so. He promised secresy, and agreed to sign the documents if the other parties did not meet their engagement.

This was about the 15th November. To all who spoke to me about the Museum, I simply remarked, that I had lost it. In the mean time the new company could not sell a dollar's worth of stock, for I kept up a perfect shower of squibs through the papers.

About the 1st of December, I received a letter from the Secretary of the Peale's Museum Company, or rather the "New-York Museum Company," as it was called, desiring me to meet the directors on the following Monday morning at the Museum, when and where I should probably hear something to my advantage. I saw that the newspaper medicine was doing its office. It was evident that those gentlemen wished to purchase my silence.

I was punctual at the meeting. The "honorable board of directors" was in session. The venerable President, a gray-haired, hawk-eyed old man, who had recently been President of a broken bank, accosted me with his blandest smile and smoothest tone of language. The upshot of the matter was, they proposed to hire me to manage the united museums. I professed to take it all in earnest, and when asked to mention the salary I should expect, I specified $3000 per annum. They complimented me on my character for ability in that department, and engaged me at the sum I demanded, my salary to commence on the 1st day of

January, 1842. As I was leaving the "august presence," the amiable President pleasantly remarked, "Of course, Mr. Barnum, we shall have no more of your squibs through the newspapers."

"I ever try to serve the interests of my employers," I replied.

The jolly directors probably had a hearty laugh so soon as I was beyond hearing their unseemly mirth. They probably meant by thus keeping me quiet to sell their stock, and permit the stock-holders to throw me overboard as soon as they pleased. They thought they had caught me securely. I *knew* that I had caught *them*.

Finding that I was now removed out of the way, those directors did not fear that any other person would attempt to buy the American Museum, and they concluded not to advertise their stock until the first of January, as that would give the people longer time to forget the attacks which I had made on it. As for their promised payment on the 26th December, unaware that Mr. Heath had contracted to me for $12,000, they thought he would cheerfully wait on them until it suited their pleasure to pay him. In fact, so unconcerned were they upon this point, that they did not even call on the administrator on the 26th inst., nor send him the slightest apology for not doing so!

On the morning of the 27th, I was at Mr. Olmsted's apartment, with my legal counsellor, Chas. T. Cromwell, Esq., at half-past nine o'clock. Mr. Heath came with his lawyer punctually at ten, and before two o'clock that day I was put in formal possession of the American Museum. The first act which I performed, after being thus installed, was to write and dispatch the following note:

American Museum, New-York, Dec. 27, 1841.
To the President and Directors of the New-York Museum:
Gentleman:—It gives me great pleasure to inform you that you are placed upon the Free List of this establishment until further notice.
P. T. Barnum, Proprietor.

The President was astonished beyond measure, and could scarcely believe his eyes. He called upon Mr. Heath, and learned that I had indeed bought and was in possession of the American Museum. His indignation knew no bounds. He threatened him with a prosecution, but finding that this availed him nothing, he demanded the return of the thousand dollars which had been paid on the agreement. It was refused because forfeited, and the company lost it.

No one will doubt that I now put forth all my energy. It was strictly "neck or nothing." I must either pay for the establishment within a stipulated period, or forfeit it, including all I might have paid on account, provided Mr. Olmsted should insist on the letter of the contract. Let "come what would," I was determined to *deserve* success, and brain and hands and feet were alike busy in forwarding the interests of the Museum.

The system of economy necessary to support my family in the city of New-York upon $600 a year, was not only assented to by my treasure of a wife, but she expressed her willingness to reduce the expenses to four hundred dollars per year, if necessary.

One day, about six months after I had purchased the Museum, my friend Mr. Olmsted happened in at my ticket office about twelve o'clock, and found me alone eating my dinner, which consisted of a few slices of corned beef and bread that I had brought from home in the morning. "Is this the way you eat your dinner?" he inquired.

"I have not eaten a warm dinner since I bought the Museum, except on the Sabbath," I replied, "and I intend never to eat another on a week-day until I am out of debt."

"Ah! you are safe, and will pay for the Museum before the year is out," he replied, clapping me familiarly on the shoulder. And he was right, for in less than a year from that period, I was in full possession of the Museum as my own property, every cent having been paid out of the profits of the establishment.

The American Museum, at the date of my purchase, was little more than the nucleus of what it is now. During the thirteen years of my proprietorship, I have considerably more than doubled the value of the permanent attractions and curiosities of the establishment. The additions were derived, partly from Peale's Museum, (which I bought and transferred to my former collection in the fall of 1842;) partly from the large and rare collection known as the Chinese Museum, (which I removed to the American Museum in 1848;) and partly by purchases wherever I could find curiosities, in both America and Europe.

The space now occupied for my Museum purposes is more than double what it was in 1841. The Lecture Room, which was originally narrow, ill-contrived and uncomfortable, has been several times enlarged and improved, and at present may be pronounced one of the most commodious and beautiful halls of entertainment in New-York.

There have been enlargement and improvement in other respects. At first, the Museum was merely a collection of curiosities by day, and in the evening there was a performance, consisting of disjointed and disconnected amusements, such as are still to be found at many of the inferior shows. Saturday *afternoon* was soon appropriated to performances, and shortly afterwards the *afternoon* of Wednesday was added. The programme has for years included the afternoon and evening of every day in the week, (of course excepting the Sabbath,) and on great holidays, we have sometimes given as many as twelve performances.

There has been a gradual change in these, and the transient attractions of the Museum have been greatly diversified. Industrious fleas, educated dogs, jugglers, automatons, ventriloquists, living statuary, tableaux, gipsies, albinoes, fat boys, giants, dwarfs, rope-dancers, caricatures of phrenology, and "live Yankees," pantomime, instrumental music, singing and dancing in great variety, (including Ethiopians,) etc. Dioramas, panoramas, models of Dublin, Paris, Niagara, Jerusalem, etc., mechanical figures, fancy glassblowing, knitting machines and other triumphs in the mechanical arts, dissolving views, American Indians, including their warlike and religious ceremonies enacted on the stage, etc., etc.

I need not specify the order of time in which these varieties were presented to the public. In one respect there has been a thorough though gradual change in the general plan, for the *moral drama*[22] is now, and has been for several years, the principal feature of the Lecture Room of the American Museum.

Apart from the merit and interest of these performances, and apart from every thing connected with the stage, my permanent collection of curiosities is, without doubt, abundantly worth the uniform charge of admission to all the entertainments of the establishment, and I can therefore afford to be accused of "humbug" when I add such transient novelties as increase its attractions. If I have exhibited a questionable dead mermaid in my Museum, it should not be overlooked that I have also exhibited cameleopards, a rhinoceros, grisly bears, orang-outangs, great serpents, etc., about which there could be no mistake because they were alive; and I should hope that a little "clap-trap" occasionally, in the way of transparencies, flags, exaggerated pictures, and puffing advertisements, might find an offset in a wilderness of wonderful, instructive, and amusing realities. Indeed I cannot doubt that the sort of "clap-trap" here referred to, is allowable, and that the public like a little of it mixed up with the great realities which I provide. The titles of "humbug," and the "prince of humbugs," were first applied to me by myself. I made these titles a part of my "stock in trade," and may here quote a passage from the "Fortunes of the Scattergood Family," a work by the popular English writer, Albert Smith:

[22]A theatrical performance that promoted temperance or other causes espoused by evangelical reformers at this time.

"'It's a great thing to be a humbug,' said Mr. Rossett. 'I've been called so often. It means hitting the public in reality. Anybody who can do so, is sure to be called a humbug by somebody who can't.'"

Among my first extra exhibitions produced at the American Museum, was a model of the Falls of Niagara, belonging to Grain the artist. It was undoubtedly a fine model, giving the mathematical proportions of that great cataract, and the trees, rocks, buildings, etc., in its vicinity. But the absurdity of the thing consisted in introducing water, thus pretending to present a *fac simile* of that great wonder of nature. The falls were about eighteen inches high, every thing else being in due proportion!

I confess I felt somewhat ashamed of this myself, yet it made a good line in the bill, and I bought the model for $200. My advertisements then announced among the attractions of the Museum,

THE GREAT MODEL OF NIAGARA FALLS,
WITH REAL WATER!

A single barrel of water answered the purpose of this model for an entire season; for the falls flowed into a reservoir behind the scenes, and the water was continually re-supplied to the cataract by means of a small pump.

Many visitors who could not afford to travel to Niagara, were doubtless induced to visit the "model with real water," and if they found it rather "small potatoes," they had the whole Museum to fall back upon for 25 cents, and no fault was found.

One day I was peremptorily summoned to appear before the Board of Croton Water Commissioners the next morning at ten o'clock. I was punctual.

"Sir," said the President, "you pay only $25 per annum for the Croton water at the Museum. That is simply intended to supply the ordinary purposes of your establishment. We cannot furnish water for your Niagara Falls without large extra compensation."

Begging "his honor" not to believe all he read in the papers, nor to be too literal in the interpretation of my large showbills, I explained the operation of the great cataract, and offered to pay a dollar a drop for all the water I used for Niagara Falls exceeding one barrel per month, provided my pump continued in good order! I was permitted to retire, amid a hearty burst of laughter from the Commissioners, in which his honor the President condescended to join. . . .

The "Fejee Mermaid" was by many supposed to be a curiosity manufactured by myself, or made to my order. This is not the fact. I certainly had much to do in bringing it before the public, and as I am now in the confessional mood, I will "make a clean breast" of the ways and means I adopted for that purpose. I must first, however, relate how it came into my possession and its alleged history.

Early in the summer of 1842, Moses Kimball, Esq., the popular proprietor of the Boston Museum, came to New-York and exhibited to me what purported to be a mermaid. He stated that he had bought it of a sailor whose father, while in Calcutta in 1817 as captain of a Boston ship, (of which Captain John Ellery was principal owner,) had purchased it, believing it to be a preserved specimen of a veritable mermaid, obtained, as he was assured, from Japanese sailors. Not doubting that it would prove as surprising to others as it had been to himself, and hoping to make a rare speculation of it as an extraordinary curiosity, he appropriated $6000 of the ship's money to the purchase of it, left the ship in charge of the mate, and went to London.

He did not realize his expectations, and returned to Boston. Still believing that his curiosity was a genuine animal and therefore highly valuable, he preserved it with great care, not stinting himself in the expense of keeping it insured, though re-engaged as ship's captain under his former employers to reimburse the sum taken from their funds to pay for the mermaid. He died possessing no other property, and his only son and heir, who placed a low estimate on his father's purchase, sold it to Mr. Kimball, who brought it to New-York for my inspection.

Such was the story. Not trusting my own acuteness on such matters, I requested my naturalist's opinion of the *genuineness* of the animal. He replied that he could not conceive how it was manufactured; for he never knew a monkey with such peculiar teeth, arms, hands, etc., nor had he knowledge of a fish with such peculiar fins.

"Then why do you suppose it is manufactured?" I inquired.

"Because I don't believe in mermaids," replied the naturalist.

"That is no reason at all," said I, "and therefore I'll believe in the mermaid, and hire it."

This was the easiest part of the experiment. How to modify general incredulity in the existence of mermaids, so far as to awaken curiosity to see and examine the specimen, was now the all-important question. Some extraordinary means must be resorted to, and I saw no better method than to "start the ball a-rolling" at some distance from the centre of attraction.

In due time a communication appeared in the New-York Herald, dated and mailed in Montgomery, Ala., giving the news of the day, trade, the crops, political gossip, etc., and also an incidental paragraph about a certain Dr. Griffin, agent of the Lyceum of Natural History in London, recently from Pernambuco, who had in his possession a most remarkable curiosity, being nothing less than a veritable mermaid taken among the Fejee Islands, and preserved in China, where the Doctor had bought it at a high figure for the Lyceum of Natural History.

A week or ten days afterwards, a letter of similar tenor, dated and mailed in Charleston, S.C., varying of course in the items of local news, was published in another New-York paper.

This was followed by a third letter, dated and mailed in Washington city, published in still another New-York paper—there being in addition the expressed hope that the editors of the Empire City would beg a sight of the extraordinary curiosity before Dr. Griffin took ship for England.

A few days subsequently to the publication of this thrice-repeated announcement, Mr. Lyman (who was my employee in the case of Joice Heth) was duly registered at one of the principal hotels in Philadelphia as Dr. Griffin of Pernambuco for London. His gentlemanly, dignified, yet social manners and liberality gained him a fine reputation in a few days, and when he paid his bill one afternoon, preparatory to leaving for New-York the next day, he expressed his thanks to the landlord for special attention and courtesy. "If you will step to my room," said Lyman, alias Griffin, "I will permit you to see something that will surprise you." Whereupon the landlord was shown the most extraordinary curiosity in the world—a mermaid. He was so highly gratified and interested that he earnestly begged permission to introduce certain friends of his, including several editors, to view the wonderful specimen.

"Although it is no interest of mine," said the curiosity-hunter, "the Lyceum of Natural History, of which I am agent, will not be injured by granting the courtesy you request." And so an appointment was made for the evening.

The result might easily be gathered from the editorial columns of the Philadelphia papers a day or two subsequently to that interview with the mermaid. Suffice it to say, that the plan worked admirably, and the Philadelphia press aided the press of New-York in awakening a wide-reaching and increasing curiosity to see the mermaid.

I may as well confess that those three communications from the South were written by myself, and forwarded to friends of mine, with instructions respectively to mail them, each on the day of its date. This fact and the corresponding post-marks did much to prevent suspicion of a hoax, and the New-York editors thus unconsciously contributed to my arrangements for bringing the mermaid into public notice.

Lyman then returned to New-York with his precious treasure, and putting up at the Pacific Hotel in Greenwich street as Dr. Griffin, it soon reached the ears of the wide-awake reporters for the press that the mermaid was in town. They called at the Pacific Hotel, and the polite agent of the British Lyceum of Natural History kindly permitted them to gratify their curiosity. The New-York newspapers contained numerous reports of these examinations, all of which were quite satisfactory.

I am confident that the reporters and editors who examined this animal were honestly persuaded that it was what it purported to be — a veritable mermaid. Nor is this to be wondered at, since, if it was a work of art, the monkey and fish were so nicely conjoined that no human eye could detect the point where the junction was formed. The spine of the fish proceeded in a straight and apparently unbroken line to the base of the skull — the hair of the animal was found growing several inches down on the shoulders of the fish, and the application of a microscope absolutely revealed what seemed to be minute fish scales lying in myriads amidst the hair. The teeth and formation of the fingers and hands differed materially from those of any monkey or orang-outang ever discovered, while the location of the fins was different from those of any species of the fish tribe known to naturalists. The animal was an ugly, dried-up, black-looking, and diminutive specimen, about three feet long. Its mouth was open. its tail turned over, and its arms thrown up, giving it the appearance of having died in great agony.

Assuming, what is no doubt true, that the mermaid was manufactured, it was a most remarkable specimen of ingenuity and untiring patience. For my own part I really had scarcely cared at the time to form an opinion of the origin of this creature, but it was my impression that it was the work of some ingenious Japanese, Chinaman, or other eastern genius, and that it had probably been one among the many hideous objects of Buddhist or Hindoo worship. . . .

While Lyman was preparing public opinion on mermaids at the Pacific Hotel, I was industriously at work (though of course privately) in getting up wood-cuts and transparencies, as well as a pamphlet, proving the authenticity of mermaids, all in anticipation of the speedy exhibition of Dr. Griffin's specimen. I had three several and distinct pictures of mermaids engraved, and with a peculiar description written for each, had them inserted in 10,000 copies of the pamphlet which I had printed and quietly stored away in a back office until the time came to use them.

I then called respectively on the editors of the New-York Herald, and two of the Sunday papers, and tendered to each the free use of a mermaid cut, with a well-written description, for their papers of the ensuing Sunday. I informed each editor that I had hoped to use this cut in showing the Fejee Mermaid, but since Mr. Griffin had announced that as agent for the Lyceum of Natural History, he could not permit it to be exhibited in America, my chance seemed dubious, and therefore he was welcome to the use of the engraving and description. The three mermaids made their appearance in the three different papers on the morning of Sunday, July 17, 1842.

Each editor supposed he was giving his readers an exclusive treat in the mermaid line, but when they came to discover that I had played the same game with the three different papers, they pronounced it a *scaly* trick.

The mermaid fever was now getting pretty well up. Few city readers had missed seeing at least one of the illustrations, and as the several printed descriptions made direct allusion to *the* mermaid of Mr. Griffin now in town, a desire to see it was generally prevailing. My 10,000 mermaid pamphlets were then put into the hands of boys, and sold at a penny each, (half the cost,) in all the principal hotels, stores, etc., etc.

When I thought the public was thoroughly "posted up" on the subject of mermaids, I sent an agent to engage Concert Hall, Broadway, for the exhibition. . . .

A large number of visitors attended Concert Hall, and Lyman, alias Griffin, exhibited the mermaid with much dignity. I could not help fearing that some of the Joice Heth victims would discover in Professor Griffin the exhibitor of the "nurse of Washington," but happily no such catastrophe occurred. Lyman, surrounded by numerous connecting links in nature, as set forth in the advertisement, and with the hideous-looking mermaid firmly secured from the hands of visitors by a glass vase, enlightened his audiences by curious accounts of his travels and adventures, and by scientific harangues upon the works of nature in general, and mermaids in particular.

The public appeared to be satisfied, but as some persons always *will* take things literally, and make no allowance for poetic license even in mermaids, an occasional visitor, after having seen the large transparency in front of the hall, representing a beautiful creature half woman and half fish, about eight feet in length, would be slightly surprised in finding that the reality was a black-looking specimen of dried monkey and fish that a boy a few years old could easily run away with under his arm.

The mermaid remained a single week at Concert Hall, and was then advertised to be seen at the American Museum, " without extra charge." Numerous transparencies had been prepared; show-bills were posted with a liberal hand; and on Monday morning, a flag representing a mermaid eighteen feet in length was streaming directly in front of the Museum. Lyman saw it as he was slowly approaching to commence operations. He quickened his pace, entered my office, and demanded, "What in the name of all conscience is that immense flag out for?"

"In order that nobody shall enter Broadway without knowing where to find the mermaid," I replied.

"Well, that flag must come in. Nobody can satisfy the public with our dried-up specimen *eighteen inches* long, after exhibiting a picture representing it as *eighteen feet*. It is preposterous."

"Oh, nonsense," I replied; "that is only to catch the eye. They don't expect to see a mermaid of that size."

"I tell you it won't do," replied Lyman, "I think I ought to know something of the public 'swallow' by this time, and I tell you the mermaid won't go down if that flag remains up."

"That flag cost me over seventy dollars, and it must remain up," I replied.

Lyman deliberately buttoned his coat, and said as he slowly walked towards the door, "Well, Mr. Barnum, if you like to fight under that flag, you can do so, but *I* won't."

"What! you are a deserter, then!" I replied, laughing.

"Yes, I desert false colors when they are too strong," said Lyman; "and *you* will desert them before night," he continued.

I could not spare "Professor Griffin," and was reluctantly compelled to take down the flag. It never saw the light again.

The mermaid was afterwards exhibited in various parts of the country, and finally returned to its owner, Mr. Kimball, who has ever since given it a prominent niche in his truly beautiful and attractive "Boston Museum." ...

That "her ladyship" was an attractive feature, may be inferred from these facts and figures:

The receipts of the American Museum for the four weeks immediately preceding the exhibition of the mermaid, amounted to $1272. During the first four weeks of the mermaid's exhibition, the receipts amounted to $3341.93.

The New-York Museum Company, having failed in selling their stock, let their establishment, known as Peale's Museum, to Yankee Hill. After a management of a few months, he failed. Mr. Henry Bennett then took charge of it, reduced the price to one "York shilling,"[23] and endeavored to thrive by burlesquing whatever I produced. Thus, when I exhibited the Fejee Mermaid, he stuck a codfish and monkey together and advertised the *Fudg-ee* Mermaid. When I announced a company of talented vocalists, well known as the "Orphean Family," Bennett advertised the "*Orphan* Family." It was an invention creditable to his genius, and created some laughter at my expense, but it also served to draw attention to my Museum.

After the novelty of Bennett's opposition died away, he did a losing business, and on the 2d of January, 1843, he closed his Museum, having lost his last dollar. The entire collection fell into the hands of the proprietor of the building, on a claim of arrearages of rent amounting to six or eight thousand dollars. I purchased it privately for $7000, cash, hired the building, and secretly engaging Bennett as my agent, we run a spirited opposition. I found profit in the arrangement by attracting public attention, and at the end of six months, the whole establishment, including the splendid Gallery of American Portraits, was transferred to my American Museum.

I do not here intend to disparage Bennett's ability nor to glorify my own. Independently of any thing personal to either of us, I had superior advantages; and if the result of the real strife between us had at any time been doubtful, my lucky stars soon put me in possession of a means of overwhelming all opposition.

Being in Albany on business in November, 1842, the Hudson River was frozen tight, and I returned to New-York by way of the Housatonic Railroad. I stopped one night in Bridgeport, Ct., my brother, Philo F., keeping the Franklin Hotel at the time.

I had heard of a remarkably small child in Bridgeport; and by my request my brother brought him to the hotel. He was the smallest child I ever saw that could walk alone. He was not two feet in height, and weighed less than sixteen pounds. He was a bright-eyed little fellow, with light hair and ruddy cheeks, was perfectly healthy, and as symmetrical as an Apollo. He was exceedingly bashful, but after some coaxing he was induced to converse with me, and informed me that his name was Charles S. Stratton, son of Sherwood E. Stratton.

He was only five years old, and to exhibit a dwarf of that age might provoke the question, How do you know that he *is* a dwarf? Some license

[23]Slang for 12 ½ cents, or half a quarter.

might indeed be taken with the facts, but even with this advantage I really felt that the adventure was nothing more than an experiment, and I engaged him for the short term of *four weeks at three dollars per week*—all/charges, including travelling and boarding of himself and mother, being at my expense.

They arrived in New-York on Thanksgiving Day, Dec. 8, 1842, and Mrs. Stratton was greatly astonished to find her son heralded in my Museum bills as Gen. Tom Thumb, a dwarf of eleven years of age, just arrived from England!

This announcement contained two deceptions. I shall not attempt to justify them, but may be allowed to plead the circumstances in extenuation. The boy was undoubtedly a dwarf, and I had the most reliable evidence that he had grown little, if any, since he was six months old; but had I announced him as only five years of age, it would have been impossible to excite the interest or awaken the curiosity of the public. The thing I aimed at was, to assure them that he was *really a dwarf*—and in *this*, at least, they were not deceived.

It was of no consequence, in reality, where he was born or where he came from, and if the announcement that he was *a foreigner* answered my purpose, the people had only themselves to blame if they did not get their money's worth when they visited the exhibition. I had observed (and sometimes, as in the case of Vivalla, had taken advantage of) the American fancy for European exotics; and if the deception, practised for a season in my dwarf experiment, has done any thing towards checking our disgraceful preference for foreigners, I may readily be pardoned for the offence I here acknowledge.

I took great pains to train my diminutive prodigy, devoting many hours to that purpose, by day and by night, and succeeded, because he had native talent and an intense love of the ludicrous. He became very fond of me. I was, and yet am, sincerely attached to him, and I candidly believe him at this moment to be the most interesting and extraordinary natural curiosity of which the world has any knowledge.

Four weeks expired, and I re-engaged him for a year at seven dollars per week, (and a gratuity of fifty dollars at the end of the agreement,) with privilege of exhibition in any section of the United States. His parents were to accompany him, and I was to pay all travelling expenses. Long before the year was out, I voluntarily increased his weekly salary to $25—and he fairly earned it, for he speedily became a public favorite. I frequently exhibited him for successive weeks in my Museum, and when I wished to introduce fresh novelties there, I sent him to numerous cities and towns in many of the States, accompanied by my friend Fordyce Hitchcock.

In the mean time, I had entirely paid for the American Museum, and entered into an agreement with Gen. Tom Thumb for his services another year, at fifty dollars per week and all expenses, with the privilege of exhibition in Europe.

X. EUROPEAN TOUR—TOM THUMB

On Thursday, January 18, 1844, I stepped on board the new and splendid packet ship *Yorkshire*, Capt. D. G. Bailey, bound for Liverpool. My party consisted of Gen. Tom Thumb, both his parents, his tutor, Professor Guillaudeu the French naturalist, and myself. The City Brass Band kindly volunteered to escort us to Sandy Hook, and we were accompanied by many of our personal friends.

At half-past one o'clock, the bell of one of the steamers that towed our ship down the bay, announced the hour of separation. There was the usual bustle, the rapidly-spoken yet often-repeated words of farewell, the cordial grip of friendship—and I acknowledge that I was decidedly in "the melting mood."

My name has so long been used in connection with incidents of the mirthful kind, that many persons, probably, do not suspect that I am susceptible of sorrowful emotion, and possibly the general tenor of these pages may confirm the suspicion. No doubt my natural bias is to merriment, and I have encouraged my inclination to "comedy," because enough of "tragedy" will force itself upon the attention of every one in spite of his efforts to the contrary; yet I should be either more or less than human, were I incapable of serious thought, or did I not frequently indulge in the sober meditation which becomes the solemn realities of life.

I do not now refer only to scenes of parting with friendly, or of leaving country and home for a few months, or even years, but I speak of the ordinary occasions of experience. I have had, and hope always to have, my seasons of loneliness and even sadness; and, though many people may not see how my profession of "a showman" can be made to appear consistent with my profession of another kind, I must claim having always revered the Christian Religion. I have been indebted to Christianity for the most serene happiness of my life, and I would not part with its consolations for all things else in the world. In all my Journeys as "a showman," the Bible has been my companion, and I have repeatedly read it attentively, from beginning to end. Whether I have or have not been profited by its precepts, is a question not here to be considered; but the scriptural doctrine of the government of God and its happy issue in the life to come, has been my chief solace in affliction and sorrow, and I hope always to cherish it as my greatest treasure.

The "melting mood" was upon me, for the pathway of the ship was toward the wide sea with its deep mysteries, and my heart clung to my family and home. I successively grasped for the last time the hand of each parting friend as he passed to the tow-boat, and I could not restrain my emotion; and when the band struck up "Home, Sweet Home!" my tears flowed thick and fast.

The distance between the ship and the steamer rapidly increased. We stood on the quarter-deck, waving our handkerchiefs, and when the strains of "Yankee Doodle" floated over the waters and distinctly saluted us, we all gave three cheers, and I wept freely, overpowered as I was with mingled feelings of regret and joy. At two o'clock the pilot left us, and thus was broken the last visible living link that bound us to our country. . . .

On the eighteenth day out, the cry of "Land ho!" brought us to the deck in great glee. The snow-capped mountains of Wales soon appeared in sight, and in three hours we were safely in the Liverpool docks. A large throng of persons were gathered upon the wharves, and many were anxiously inquiring for Tom Thumb, as it had previously been announced in Liverpool that he would arrive in the Yorkshire. His mother managed to smuggle him on shore without being noticed, for they little thought that he was small enough to be carried in arms, like an infant. . . .

It had been my intention to proceed directly to London and begin operations at "head-quarters"—that is, at the Palace, if possible. But I learned that the royal family was in mourning because of the death of Prince Albert's father, and would not permit the approach of entertainments. My letters of introduction speedily brought me into relations of friendship with many excellent families, and I was induced to hire a hall and present the General to the public in Liverpool for a short time.

Meanwhile I had confidential advices from London that Mr. Maddox, Manager of Princess's Theatre, was coming down to witness my exhibition, with a view to making an engagement. He came privately, but I was "posted up" as to his presence and object. A friend pointed him out to me in the hall, and when I stepped up to him, and called him by name, he was "taken all a-back," and avowed his purpose in visiting Liverpool. An interview resulted in an engagement of the General for three nights at Princess's Theatre. I was unwilling to contract for a longer period, and even this short engagement, though on liberal terms was acceded to only as a means of advertisement.

The General made so decided a "hit" at Princess's Theatre, that it might have been difficult to decide *which* party was the best pleased, the spectators, the manager, or myself. The first were pleased because they could not help it; the second was pleased because he had coined money by the operation; and *I* was pleased because I had a visible guarantee of success in London. I was offered a much higher figure for a re-engagement, but my purpose had been sufficiently answered. The news was out that General Tom Thumb was on the tapis,[24] as an unparalleled curiosity, and it only remained for me to bring him before the public, "on my own book," in my own time and way.

I had taken a furnished house in Grafton street, Bond street, West End, in the centre of fashion. Lord Brougham, and half a dozen families of the blood-aristocracy and many of the gentry, were my neighbors. The house had been occupied by Lord Talbot for several years previously. From this magnificent mansion, I sent letters of invitation to the editors and several of the nobility, to visit the General. Most of them called, and were highly gratified. The word of approval was indeed so passed around in high circles, that uninvited parties drove to my door in crested carriages, *and were not admitted.*

This procedure, though in some measure a stroke of policy, was not either singular or hazardous, under the circumstances. I had not yet announced a public exhibition, and as a private American gentleman it became me to maintain the dignity of my position. I therefore instructed my servant, dressed in the tinselled and powdered style of England, to deny admission to my mansion to see my "ward," excepting to persons who brought cards of invitation. He did it in a proper manner, and no offence could be taken—though I was always particular to send an invitation immediately to such as had not been admitted.

During our first week in London, Mr. Everett, the American Minister, to whom I had letters of introduction, called and was highly pleased with his diminutive though renowned countryman. We dined with him the next day, by invitation, and his family loaded the young American with presents. Mr. Everett kindly promised to use influence at the Palace in person, with a view to having Tom Thumb introduced to Her Majesty Queen Victoria.

A few evenings afterwards the Baroness Rothschild sent her carriage for us. Her mansion is a noble structure in Piccadilly, surrounded by a high wall, through the gate of which our carriage was driven and brought up in front of the main entrance. Here we were received by

[24]A Victorian saying meaning "under consideration."

half a dozen servants elegantly dressed in black coats and pantaloons, white vests and cravats, white kid gloves, and, in fact, wearing the *tout ensemble* of gentlemen. One old chap was dressed in livery — a heavy laced coat, breeches, a large, white powdered and curled wig, and every thing else to match. The hall was brilliantly illuminated, and each side was graced with the most beautiful statuary. We were ushered up a broad flight of marble stairs, and our names announced at the door of the drawing-room by an elegantly-dressed servant, who under other circumstances I might have supposed was a member of the noble family.

As we entered the drawing-room, a glare of magnificence met my sight which it is impossible for me to describe. The Baroness was seated on a gorgeous couch covered with rich figured silk damask, (there were several similar couches in the room,) and several lords and ladies were seated in chairs elegantly carved and covered with gold, looking indeed like solid gold, except the bottoms, which were rich velvet. On each side of the mantlepiece were specimens of marble statuary — on the right of which stood glazed cabinets containing urns, vases, and a thousand other things of the most exquisite workmanship, made of gold, silver, diamonds, alabaster, pearl, etc. The centre table, and several tables about the size and something like the shape of a pianoforte, all covered with gold, or made of ebony thickly inlaid with pearls of various hues, were loaded with *bijous* of every kind, surpassing in elegance any thing I had ever dreamed of. The chairs at one end of the room were made of ebony, inlaid with pearl and gold, elegantly cushioned with damask. The walls were panelled and heavily gilt — the curtains and ornaments of the most costly kind. The immense chandeliers, candelabras, etc., exceeded all my powers of description; and I confess my total inability to give a correct idea of the splendor in which lived the wife of the most wealthy banker in the world.

Here we spent about two hours. About twenty lords and ladies were present. On taking our leave, an elegant and well-filled purse was quietly slipped into my hand, and I felt that the golden shower was beginning to fall!

It could not be a delusion, for precisely the same trick was played upon me shortly afterwards, at the mansion of Mr. Drummond, another eminent banker.

I now engaged the "Egyptian Hall," in Piccadilly, and the announcement of my unique exhibition was promptly answered by a rush of visitors, in which the wealth and fashion of London were liborally represented.

I made these arrangements because I had little hope of being soon brought to the Queen's presence, (for the reason before mentioned,) but Mr. Everett's generous influence secured my object. I breakfasted at his house one morning, by invitation, in company with Mr. Charles Murray, an author of creditable repute, who held the office of Master of the Queen's Household.

In the course of conversation, Mr. Murray inquired as to my plans, and I informed him that I intended going to the Continent shortly, though I should be glad to remain if the General could have an interview with the Queen — adding that such an event would be of great consequence to me.

Mr. Murray kindly offered his good offices in the case, and soon afterwards one of the Life Guards, a tall noble-looking fellow, bedecked as became his station, brought me a note, conveying the Queen's invitation to General Tom Thumb and his guardian, Mr. Barnum, to appear at Buckingham Palace on an evening specified. Special instructions were the same day orally given me by Mr. Murray, by Her Majesty's command, to suffer the General to appear before her, as he would appear anywhere else, without any training in the use of the titles of royalty, as the Queen desired to see him act naturally and without restraint.

Determined to make the most of the occasion, I put a placard on the door of the Egyptian Hall: "Closed this evening, General Tom Thumb being at Buckingham Palace by command of Her Majesty."

On arriving at the Palace, the Lord in Waiting put me "under drill" as to the manner and form in which I should conduct myself in the presence of royalty. I was to answer all questions by Her Majesty through *him*, and in no event to speak directly to the Queen. In leaving the royal presence I was to "back out," keeping my face always towards Her Majesty, and the illustrious Lord kindly gave me a specimen of that sort of backward locomotion. How far I profited by his instructions and example, will presently appear.

We were conducted through a long corridor to a broad flight of marble steps, which led to the Queen's magnificent picture gallery, where Her Majesty and Prince Albert, the Duchess of Kent, and twenty or thirty of the nobility, were awaiting our arrival. They were standing at the farther end of the room when the doors were thrown open, and the General toddled in, looking like a wax-doll gifted with the power of locomotion. Surprise and pleasure were depicted on the countenances of the royal circle, at beholding this *mite* of humanity so much smaller than they had evidently expected to find him.

The General advanced with a firm step, and as he came within hailing distance made a very graceful bow, and exclaimed, "Good evening, *Ladies and Gentlemen!*"

A burst of laughter followed this salutation. The Queen then took him by the hand, led him about the gallery, and asked him many questions, the answers to which kept the party in an unintermitted strain of merriment. The General familiarly informed the Queen that her picture gallery was "first-rate," and told her he should like to see the Prince of Wales. The Queen replied that the Prince had retired to rest, but that he should see him on some future occasion. The General then gave his songs, dances, imitations, etc., and after a conversation with Prince Albert and all present, which continued for more than an hour, we were permitted to depart.

Before describing the process and incidents of "backing out," I must acknowledge how sadly I broke through the counsel of the Lord in Waiting. While Prince Albert and others were engaged with Tom, the Queen was gathering information from *me* in regard to his history, etc. Two or three questions were put and answered through the process indicated in my drill. It was a round-about way of doing business not at all to my liking, and I suppose the Lord in Waiting was seriously shocked, if not outraged, when I entered directly into conversation with Her Majesty. She, however, seemed not disposed to check my boldness, for she immediately spoke directly to me in obtaining the information which she sought. I felt entirely at ease in her presence, and could not avoid contrasting her sensible and amiable manners with the stiffness and formality of upstart gentility at home or abroad.

The Queen was modestly attired in plain black, and wore no ornaments. Indeed, surrounded as she was by ladies arrayed in the highest style of magnificence, their dresses sparkling with diamonds, a stranger would have selected her as the last person in the circle who could have been the Queen of England.

The Lord in Waiting was perhaps mollified toward me when he saw me following his illustrious example in retiring from the royal presence. He was accustomed to the process, and therefore was able to keep somewhat a-head (or rather a-back) of me, but even *I* stepped rather fast for the other member of the retiring party. We had a considerable distance to travel in that long gallery before reaching the door, and whenever the General found he was losing ground, he turned around and ran a few steps, then resumed the position of "backing out," then turned around and ran, and so continued to alternate his methods of getting to the door, until the gallery fairly rang with the merriment of the royal spectators. It was really one of the richest scenes I ever saw, especially the concluding section. Running, under the circumstances, was an offence sufficiently heinous to excite the indignation of the Queen's favorite poodle-dog, and he vented his displeasure by barking so sharply as to startle the General from his propriety. He however recovered immediately, and with his little cane commenced an attack on the poodle, and a funny fight ensued, which renewed and increased the merriment of the royal party.

This was near the door of exit. We had scarcely passed into the anteroom, when one of the Queen's attendants came to us with the expressed hope of Her Majesty, that the General had sustained no damage—to which the Lord in Waiting playfully added, that in case of injury to so renowned a personage, he should fear a declaration of war by the United States!

The courtesies of the Palace were not yet exhausted, for we were escorted to an apartment in which refreshments had been provided for us. We did ample justice to the viands, though my mind was rather looking into the future than enjoying the present. I was anxious that the "Court Journal" of the ensuing day should contain more than a mere line in relation to the General's interview with the Queen, and, on inquiry, I learned that the gentleman who had charge of that portion of the daily papers was then in the Palace. He was sent for by my solicitation, and promptly acceded to my request for such a notice as would attract attention. He even generously desired me to give him an outline of what I sought, and I was pleased to see, afterwards, that he had inserted my notice *verbatim*. . . .

The British public were now fairly excited. Not to have seen General Tom Thumb was voted to be decidedly unfashionable, and from the 20th of March until the 20th of July the levees of the little General at Egyptian Hall were continually crowded—the receipts averaging during the whole period about $500 per day, sometimes going considerably beyond that sum. At the fashionable hour, between fifty and sixty carriages of the nobility have been counted at one time standing in front of our exhibition rooms in Piccadilly.

Portraits of the little General were published in all the pictorial papers of the time. Polkas and quadrilles were named after him, and songs were sung in his praise. He was an almost constant theme for the "London Punch,"[25] which served the General and myself up so daintily that it no doubt added vastly to our receipts.

[25]A popular British magazine.

The expenses of the hall were only £44 per month, and our family expenses (as we now kept house) averaged but one pound per week each. Altogether I reckon our entire disbursements, including printing, and every thing appertaining to the exhibition, at $50 per day.

Besides his three public performances per day, the little General attended from three to four private parties per week, for which we were paid eight to ten guineas each. Frequently we would visit two parties in the same evening, and the demand in that line was much greater than the supply. . . .

At the various parties which we attended, we met, in the course of the season, nearly all of the nobility. That a single member of the nobility failed to see General Tom Thumb either at their own houses, the house of a friend, or at his public levees at Egyptian Hall, I do not believe.

With some of the first personages in the land he was a great pet. Among these may be mentioned Sir Robert and Lady Peel, the Duke and Duchess of Buckingham, Duke of Bedford, Duke of Devonshire, Count d'Orsay, Lady Blessington, Daniel O'Connell, Lord Adolphus Fitzclarence, Lord Chesterfield, Mr. and Mrs. Joshua Bates, of the firm of Baring Brothers & Co., etc., etc.

We had the free entrée to all the theatres, public gardens, and places of entertainment, and frequently met the principal artists, editors, poets, and authors of the country.

Albert Smith was and is a particular friend of mine. He wrote a play for the General called "Hop o' my Thumb,"[26] which he played with great success at the Lyceum Theatre, London, and in several of the provincial theatres. We were absent from America over three years, and visited nearly every town in England and Scotland, besides Belfast and Dublin, in Ireland.* In Dublin our receipts on the last day, after having exhibited the previous week in the great Rotunda Hall, were £261, or $1305. Besides that, we received £50, or $250, for playing the same evening at the Theatre Royal. We also visited nearly every town in France, and Brussels and several other towns in Belgium, at which latter city we appeared before King Leopold and the Queen at their palace. . . .

We returned from Brussels to London, where the General again opened his "Levees" with undiminished success, and also played at the theatres in "Hop o' my Thumb." He also performed in the Surrey Zoological Gardens, under the direction of its proprietor and my particular friend, Mr. Tyler. From London we went to Scotland, stopping

---

[26]This play, based on a French fairy tale about a small boy who defeats an ogre, showcased Thumb's theatrical talents and singing abilities.

to exhibit in important places by the way, and finally all returned to America in February, 1847.

The General had been absent for somewhat more than three years, during which space, leaving him in charge of faithful agents, I had twice visited the United States. On my first visit, my wife and children returned with me to Europe, and remained nine months. My second visit to America was in April, 1846.

The first of these visits was in October, 1844. Twenty months of pecuniary prosperity appeared to have effected some change in the views or conduct of certain people regarding me—a change which I afterwards alluded to in one of my letters to the Sunday Atlas in the following terms:

"A source of great amusement to me on my return to New-York, was the discovery of many *new* friends. I could hardly credit my senses, when I discovered so many wealthy men extending their hands to me and expressing their delight at seeing me again, who before I left New-York would have looked down on me with disdain had I presumed to speak to them. I really forgot, until they forced the truth upon my mind, that since I left them I had accumulated a few more dirty dollars, and that now therefore we stood on equal ground! On the other hand, I met some honest friends in humble circumstances, who approached me with diffidence never before exhibited—and then again I felt ashamed of human nature. What a pitiful state of society it is, which elevates a booby or a tyrant to its summit, provided he has more gold than others—while a good heart or a wise head is contemptuously disregarded if their owner happens to be poor!

"No man can be truly happy who, because he chances to be rich, mounts upon stilts, and attempts to stride over his fellow-beings. For my own part, the only special benefit which, as I conceive, wealth can confer upon an individual is, that while it enables him to secure the comforts and conveniences of life, it affords him an opportunity to contribute to the wants of his fellow-beings. My sincere prayer is, that I may be reduced to beggary, rather than become a pampered, purse-proud aristocrat.

"This coat, I am sorry to say, will fit many of my acquaintances in New-York. I beg them, for their own sakes and for mine, to wear it. I wish *them* and all the world, to know that my father was *a tailor* and that I am '*a showman*' by profession, and all *the gliding* shall make nothing else of me. When a man is ashamed of his origin, or gets above his business, he is a poor devil, who merits the detestation of all who know him. The idea that a shoemaker or a tinker cannot be a gentleman, is simply ridiculous; but it is not as much so as that which assumes every man necessarily to be a gentleman if he happens to be wealthy. Money should in no sense be made the standard of respectability or honor. We should never worship 'golden calves.'" . . .

It will naturally be supposed that I promptly made use of General Tom Thumb's European reputation, on our arrival in New-York, in February, 1847. He immediately appeared in the American Museum, and for four weeks drew such crowds of visitors as had never been seen there before. He afterwards spent a month in Bridgeport, with his kindred. To prevent being annoyed by the curious who would be sure to throng the houses of his relatives, he exhibited two days at Bridgeport. The receipts, amounting to several hundred dollars, were presented to the Bridgeport Charitable Society. The Bridgeporters were much delighted to see their old friend "little Charlie" again. They little thought, when they saw him playing about the streets a few years previously, that he was destined to create such a sensation among the crowned heads of the old world; and now returning with his European reputation, he was of course a great curiosity to his former acquaintances, as well as the public generally. His Bridgeport friends found that he had not increased in size during the four and a half years of his absence, but they discovered that he had become sharp and witty, abounding in "foreign airs and native graces;" in fact, that he was quite unlike the little diffident country fellow whom they had formerly known.

"We never thought Charlie much of a phenomenon when he lived among us," said one of the first citizens of the place, but now that he has become 'Barnumized,' he is a rare curiosity."

"How old are you, General?" asked one of his acquaintances.

"As Mr. Barnum makes it out, I am fifteen," said the General, laughing, for he was aware that the inquirer knew his true age to be only nine!

I was surprised to find that I had also become a curiosity during my absence. If I showed myself about the Museum or wherever else I was known, I found eyes peering and fingers pointing at me, and could frequently overhear the remark, "There's Barnum," "That's old Barnum," etc. By the way, I can't understand how it is that most people whom I do not know, and many whom I do, will insist upon calling me "*Old* Barnum." I am now but forty-four years of age, and I have been called "old Barnum" these ten years.

On one occasion, soon after my return from abroad, I was sitting in the ticket-office reading a newspaper. A man came and purchased a ticket of admission. "Is Barnum in the Museum?" he asked. The ticket-seller, pointing to me, answered, "This is Mr. Barnum." Supposing the gentleman had business with me, I looked up from the paper. "Is this Mr. Barnum?" he asked. "It is," I replied. He stared at me for a moment, and then, throwing down his ticket, he exclaimed, "It's all right. I have got the worth of my money;" and away he went, without going into the Museum at all! . . .

XI. THE JENNY LIND ENTERPRISE

In October, 1849, I first conceived the idea of bringing Jenny Lind to this country. I had never heard her sing, inasmuch as she arrived in London a few weeks after I quitted it with General Tom Thumb. Her reputation, however, was sufficient for me. I usually jump at conclusions, and almost invariably find that my first impressions are the most correct. It struck me, when I first thought of this speculation, that if properly managed it must prove immensely profitable, provided I could engage the "Swedish Nightingale"[27] on any terms within the range of reason. As it was a great undertaking, I considered the matter seriously for several days, and all my "cipherings" and calculations gave but one result—immense success.

Reflecting that very much would depend upon the manner in which she should be brought before the public, I saw that my task would be an exceedingly arduous one. It was possible, I knew, that circumstances might occur which would make the enterprise disastrous. "The public" is a very strange animal, and although a good knowledge of human nature will generally lead a caterer of amusements to hit the people right, they are fickle, and ofttimes perverse. A slight misstep in the management of a public entertainment, frequently wrecks the most promising enterprise. Taking all things into the account, I arrived at the following conclusions:

1st. The chances were greatly in favor of immense pecuniary success; and 2d. Inasmuch as my name has long been associated with "humbug," and the American public suspect that my capacities do not extend beyond the power to exhibit a stuffed monkey-skin or a dead mermaid, I can afford to lose fifty thousand dollars in such an enterprise as bringing

[27]Lind's nickname. Lind, born in Sweden in 1820, had become a singing sensation in Europe by this time.

to this country, in the zenith of her life and celebrity, the greatest musical wonder in the world, provided the engagement is carried out with credit to the management.

I thought that the sum above named would be amply sufficient to cover all possible loss, and, caring little for the personal anxiety and labor which I must necessarily encounter, I cast about for the purpose of finding the proper agent to dispatch to Europe to engage the "divine Jenny," if possible.

I found in Mr. John Hall Wilton, an Englishman who had visited this country with the Sax-Horn Players, the best man whom I knew for that purpose. . . .

The gist of all my instructions to Wilton (public and private) amounted to this: He was to engage Jenny *on shares*, if possible, so that my risk would be inconsiderable, unless he could secure her for one hundred nights for the sum of sixty thousand dollars, which terms I preferred to that of sharing. I however authorized him, if he could do no better, to engage her for one hundred and fifty nights for the sum of one hundred and fifty thousand dollars and all her expenses, including servants, carriages, secretary, etc., besides also engaging such musical assistants, not exceeding three in number, as she should select — let the terms be what they might. If necessary, I should place the entire amount of money named in the engagement in the hands of London bankers before Jenny sailed.

Wilton's compensation was arranged on a kind of sliding scale, to be governed by the terms which he made for me — so that the farther he kept below my utmost limits, the better he should be paid for making the engagements.

Wilton proceeded to London, and opened a correspondence with Miss Lind, who was then on the Continent. He learned from the tenor of her letters, that if she could be induced to visit America at all, she must be accompanied by Mr. Julius Benedict, the accomplished composer, pianist, and musical director, and also that she was impressed with the belief that Signor Belletti, the fine baritone, would be of essential service. Wilton therefore at once called upon Mr. Benedict and also Signor Belletti, who were both then in London, and in numerous interviews was enabled to learn the terms on which they would consent to engage to visit this country with Miss Lind. . . .

I was at my Museum in Philadelphia when Wilton arrived in New-York, February 19, 1850, and he immediately telegraphed me that he had signed an engagement with Jenny Lind, by which she was to commence her concerts in America in the following September. I was somewhat startled by this sudden announcement, and feeling that the time to elapse before her arrival was so long that it would be policy to keep the engagement private for a few months, I immediately telegraphed him not to mention it to any person, and that I would meet him the next day in New-York.

When we reflect how thoroughly Jenny Lind, her musical powers, her character, and wonderful successes, are now known by all classes in this country as well as throughout the whole civilized world, it is difficult to realize that, at the time this engagement was made, she was comparatively unknown on this side the water. We can hardly credit the fact, that millions of persons in America had never heard of her, that other millions had merely read her name, but had no distinct idea of who or what she was. Only a small portion of the public were really aware of her great musical triumphs in the old world, and this portion was confined almost entirely to musical people, travellers who had visited the old world, and the conductors of the press.

The next morning I started for New-York. On arriving at Princeton, we met the cars, and, purchasing the morning papers, I was overwhelmed with surprise and dismay to find in them a full account of my engagement with Jenny. However, this premature announcement could not be recalled, and I put the best face upon the matter. Being anxious to learn how this communication would strike the public mind, I informed the gentlemanly conductor (whom I well knew) that I had made an engagement with Jenny Lind, and that she would surely visit this country in the following August.

"Jenny Lind! Is she a dancer?" asked the conductor.

I informed the gentleman who and what she was, but his question had chilled me as if his words were ice. Really, thought I, if this is all that a man in the capacity of a railroad conductor between Philadelphia and New-York knows of the greatest songstress in the world, I am not sure that six months will be too long a time for me to occupy in enlightening the entire public in regard to her merits.

I had an interview with Wilton, and learned from him that, in accordance with the agreement, it would be requisite for me to place the entire amount stipulated, $187,500, in the hands of the London bankers. I instantly resolved to ratify the agreement, and immediately sent the necessary documents to Miss Lind and Messrs. Benedict and Belletti.

I then commenced preparing the public mind through the newspapers for the reception of the great songstress. . . .

The people soon began to talk about Jenny Lind, and I was particularly anxious to obtain a good portrait of her. Fortunately, a fine opportunity occurred. One day, while I was sitting in the office of the Museum, a foreigner approached me with a small package under his arm. He informed me in broken English that he was a Swede. He said he was an artist, and had just arrived from Stockholm, where Jenny Lind had kindly given him a number of sittings, and he now had with him the portrait of her which he had painted upon copper. He unwrapped the package, and showed me a beautiful picture of the Swedish Nightingale, inclosed in an elegant gilt frame, about fourteen by twenty inches. It was just the thing I wanted. His price was $50. I purchased it at once. Upon showing it to an artistic friend the same day, he quietly assured me that it was a cheap lithograph pasted on a tin back, neatly varnished, and made to appear like a fine oil painting to a novice in the arts like myself. The intrinsic value of the picture did not exceed 37 ½ cents! . . .

On Wednesday morning, August 21, 1850, Jenny Lind and Messrs. Benedict and Belletti departed from Liverpool in the steamship Atlantic, in which I had long before engaged the necessary accommodations, and on board of which I had shipped a piano for their use. They were accompanied by my agent, Wilton, also by Miss Ahmansen and Mr. Hjortzberg, cousins of Miss Lind, the latter being her secretary, also by her two servants, and the valet of Messrs. Benedict and Belletti.

It was expected that the steamer would arrive on Sunday, September 1, but, determined to meet the songstress on her arrival whenever it might be, I went to Staten Island on Saturday night, and slept at the hospitable residence of my friend, Dr. A. Sidney Doane, who was at that time the Health Officer of the port of New-York. A few minutes before twelve o'clock on Sunday morning, the Atlantic hove in sight, and immediately afterwards, through the kindness of my friend Doane, I was on board the ship, and had taken Jenny Lind by the hand.

After a few moments' conversation, she asked me when and where I had heard her sing.

"I never had the pleasure of seeing you before in my life," I replied.

"How is it possible that you dared risk so much money on a person whom you never heard sing?" she asked in surprise.

"I risked it on your reputation, which in musical matters I would much rather trust than my own judgment," I replied.

I may as well here state, that although I relied prominently upon Jenny Lind's reputation as a great musical *artiste*, I also took largely into my estimute of her success with all classes of the American public, her character for extraordinary benevolence and generosity. Without this peculiarity in her disposition, I never would have dared make the engagement which I did, as I felt sure that there were multitudes of individuals in America who would be prompted to attend her concerts by this feeling alone.

Thousands of persons covered the shipping and piers, and other thousands had congregated on the wharf at Canal street, to see her. The wildest enthusiasm prevailed as the noble steamer approached the dock. So great was the rush on a sloop near the steamer's berth, that one man, in his zeal to obtain a good view, accidentally tumbled overboard amid the shouts of those near him. Jenny witnessed this incident, and was much alarmed. He was however soon rescued, after taking to himself a cold *duck* instead of securing a look at the Nightingale. A superb bower of green trees, decorated with beautiful flags, was discovered upon the wharf, together with two triumphal arches, on one of which was inscribed, "Welcome, Jenny Lind!" The second was surmounted by the American eagle, and bore the inscription, "Welcome to America!" These decorations were probably not produced by magic, and I do not know that I can reasonably find fault with some persons who suspected that I had a hand in their erection. My private carriage was in waiting, and Jenny Lind was escorted to it by Captain West. The rest of the musical party entered the carriage, and, mounting the box at the driver's side, I directed him to the Irving House. As a *few* of the citizens had probably seen me before, my presence on the outside of the carriage aided those who filled the windows and side-walks along the whole route in coming to the conclusion that Jenny Lind had arrived.

A reference to the journals of that day will show, that seldom before had there been such enthusiasm in the city of New-York, or indeed in America.

Within ten minutes after our arrival at the Irving House, not less than ten thousand persons had congregated around the entrance in Broadway, nor was the number diminished before nine o'clock in the evening. At her request, I dined with her that afternoon, and when, according to European custom, she prepared to pledge me in a glass of wine, she was somewhat surprised at my saying, "Miss Lind, I do not think you can ask any other favor on earth which I would not gladly grant; but I am a teetotaller, and must beg to be permitted to drink your health and happiness in a glass of cold water."

At twelve o'clock that night, she was serenaded by the New-York Musical Fund Society, numbering on that occasion two hundred musicians. They were escorted to the Irving House by about three hundred firemen in their red shirts, bearing torches. At least twenty thousand persons were present. The calls for Jenny Lind were so vehement that I led her through a window to the balcony. The loud cheers from the throng lasted for several minutes, before the serenade was permitted again to proceed.

I have here briefly intimated a portion of the incidents of Jenny Lind's first day in America. For weeks afterwards the excitement was unabated. Her rooms were thronged by visitors, including the magnates of the land in both Church and State. The carriages of the *beau monde*[28] could be seen in front of her hotel at all fashionable hours, and it was with some difficulty that I prevented the fashionables from monopolizing her altogether, and thus, as I believed, sadly marring my interests by cutting her off from the warm sympathies which she had awakened among the masses. Presents of all sorts were showered upon her. Milliners, mantua-makers,[29] and shop-keepers vied with each other in calling her attention to their wares, of which they sent her many valuable specimens, delighted if in return they could receive her autograph acknowledgment. Songs, quadrilles and polkas were dedicated to her, and poets sung in her praise. We had Jenny Lind gloves, Jenny Lind bonnets, Jenny Lind riding hats, Jenny Lind shawls, mantillas, robes, chairs, sofas, pianos — in fact, every thing was Jenny Lind.

Her movements were constantly watched, and the moment her carriage appeared at the door, it was surrounded by multitudes, eager to catch a glimpse of the Swedish Nightingale.

In looking over my "scrap-books" of extracts from the New-York papers of that day, in which all accessible details concerning her were duly chronicled, it seems almost incredible that such a degree of enthusiasm should have existed. . . .

Jenny Lind's first concert was fixed to come off at Castle Garden, on Wednesday evening, September 11, and most of the tickets were sold at auction on the Saturday and Monday previous to the concert. Genin[30] the hatter laid the foundation of his fortune by purchasing the first ticket at $225.

[28]High society.

[29]A maker of women's dresses.

[30]John Nicholas Genin, a hat maker whose shop stood near Barnum's Museum, was well-known for publicity stunts aimed at bolstering his business. Newspapers across the country reported his successful bid for the ticket, raising awareness of his brand of hats.

The proprietors of the Garden saw fit to make the usual charge of one shilling to all persons who entered the premises, yet three thousand persons were present at the auction. One thousand tickets were sold on the first day for an aggregate sum of $10,141.

On the Tuesday after her arrival I informed Miss Lind that I wished to make a slight alteration in our agreement, "What is it?" she asked in surprise.

"I am convinced," I replied, "that our enterprise will be much more successful than either of us anticipated. I wish, therefore, to stipulate that you shall always receive $1000 for each concert, besides all the expenses, as heretofore agreed on, and that after taking $5500 per night for expenses and my services, the balance shall be equally divided between us."

Jenny looked at me with astonishment. She could not comprehend my proposition. After I had repeated it, and she fully understood its import, she grasped me cordially by the hand, and exclaimed, "Mr. Barnum, you are a gentleman of honor. You are generous . . . I will sing for you as long as you please. I will sing for you in America—in Europe—anywhere!"

Upon drawing the new contract, a condition was inserted, by Miss Lind's request, that she should have the right to terminate the engagement with the one hundredth concert, instead of the hundred and fiftieth, if she should desire to do so, upon paying me $25,000.

Let it not be supposed that the increase of her compensation was wholly an act of generosity on my part. I had become convinced that there was money enough in the enterprise for all of us, and I also felt that although she should have been satisfied by my complying with the terms of the agreement, yet envious persons would doubtless endeavor to create discontent in her mind, and it would be a stroke of policy to prevent the possibility of such an occurrence.

On Tuesday, September 10, I informed Miss Lind that, judging by present appearances, her portion of the proceeds of the first concert would amount to $10,000. She immediately resolved to devote every dollar of it to charity; and, sending for Mayor Woodhull, she acted under his and my advice in selecting the various institutions among which she wished the amount to be distributed.

My arrangements of the concert room were very complete. The great *parterre* and gallery of Castle Garden were divided by imaginary lines into four compartments, each of which was designated by a lamp of a peculiar color. The tickets were printed in colors corresponding with the location which the holders were to occupy, and one hundred ushers, with rosettes and bearing wands tipped with ribbons of the same hue, enabled every individual to find his or her seat without the slightest difficulty. Every seat was of course numbered to correspond with the check, which each person retained after giving up an entrance ticket at the door. These arrangements were duly advertised, and every particular was also printed upon each ticket. In order to prevent confusion, the doors were opened at five o'clock, although the concert did not commence until eight. The consequence was, that although five thousand persons were present at the first concert, their entrance was marked with as much order and quiet as was ever witnessed in the assembling of a congregation at church. These precautions were observed at all the concerts given throughout the country under my administration, and the good order which always prevailed was the subject of numberless encomiums from the public and the press.

The reception of Jenny Lind on her first appearance, in point of enthusiasm, was probably never before equalled in the world. As Mr. Benedict led her towards the foot-light, the entire audience rose to their feet and welcomed her with three cheers, accompanied by the waving of thousands of hats and handkerchiefs. This was by far the largest audience that Jenny had ever sung before. She was evidently much agitated, but the orchestra commenced, and before she had sung a dozen notes of "Casta Diva,"[31] she began to recover her self-possession, and long before the *scena* was concluded, she was as calm as if sitting in her own drawing-room. Towards the last portion of the *cavatina*, the audience were so completely carried away by their feelings, that the remainder of the air was drowned in a perfect tempest of acclamation. Enthusiasm had been wrought to its highest pitch, but the musical powers of Jenny Lind exceeded all the brilliant anticipations which had been formed, and her triumph was complete.

At the conclusion of the concert, Jenny Lind was loudly called for, and was obliged to appear three times before the audience could be satisfied. They then called vociferously for "Barnum," and I reluctantly responded to their demand.

On this first night, Mr. Julius Benedict confirmed with the American people his European reputation, as a most accomplished conductor and musical composer; while Signor Belletti inspired an admiration which grew warmer and deeper in the minds of the American people, to the end of his career in this country.

---

[31]An opera by Vincenzo Bellini first produced in 1831.

It would seem as if the Jenny Lind mania had reached its culminating point before hearing her, and I confess that I feared the anticipations of the public were too high to be realized, and hence that there would be a reaction after the first concert, but I was happily disappointed. The transcendent musical genius of the Swedish Nightingale was superior to all the pictures which fancy could paint, and the *furore* did not attain its highest point until she had been heard. The people were in ecstasies; the powers of editorial acumen, types and ink, were inadequate to sound her praises. The Rubicon was passed. The successful issue of the Jenny Lind enterprise was established. I think there were a hundred men in New-York, the day after her first concert, who would have willingly paid me $200,000 for my contract. I received repeated offers for an eighth, a tenth, or a sixteenth, equivalent to that price. But mine had been the risk, and I was determined mine should be the triumph. So elated was I with my success, in spite of all obstacles and false prophets, that I do not think a million of dollars would have tempted me to relinquish the enterprise.

No one can imagine the amount of head-work and hand-work which I performed during the first four weeks after Jenny Lind's arrival. Anticipating much of this, I had spent some time in August at the White Mountains to recruit my energies. Of course I had not been idle during the summer. I had put innumerable means and appliances into operation for the furtherance of my object, and little did the public see of the hand that indirectly pulled at their heart-strings, preparatory to a relaxation of their purse-strings; and these means and appliances were continued and enlarged throughout the whole of that triumphal musical campaign. . . .

The great assembly at Castle Garden was not gathered by Jenny Lind's great musical genius and powers alone. She was effectually brought before the public before they had seen or heard her. She appeared in the presence of a jury already excited to enthusiasm in her behalf. She more than met their expectations, and all the means I had adopted to prepare the way were thus abundantly justified.

As a manager, I worked by setting others to work. Biographies of the Swedish Nightingale were largely circulated; "Foreign Correspondence" glorified her talents and triumphs by narratives of her benevolence; and "printer's ink" was employed, in every possible form, to put and keep Jenny Lind before the people. I am happy to say that that Press generally echoed the voice of her praise, from first to last. . . .

Jenny Lind's character for benevolence became so generally known, that her door was beset by persons asking charity, and she was in the receipt, while in the principal cities, of numerous letters, all on the same subject. Her secretary examined and responded favorably to some of them. He undertook at first to answer them all, but finally abandoned that course in despair. I knew of many instances in which she gave sums of money to applicants, varying in amount from $20, $50, $500, to $1000, and in one instance $5000, to a Swedish friend; and none but "He who seeth in secret," knows the extent of her benevolence.

One night, while giving a concert in Boston, a girl approached the ticket-office, and laying down $3 for a ticket, remarked, "There goes half a month's earnings, but I am determined to hear Jenny Lind." Her secretary heard the remark, and a few minutes afterwards coming into Jenny's room, he laughingly related to her the circumstance. "Would you know the girl again?" asked Jenny, with an earnest look. Upon receiving an affirmative reply, she placed a $20 gold-piece in his hand, and said, "Poor girl! give her that with my best compliments." . . .

The morning after our arrival in Washington, President Fillmore called, and left his card, Jenny being out. When she returned and found the token of his attention, she was in something of a flurry. "Come," said she, "we must call on the President immediately."

"Why so?" I inquired.

"Because he has called on *me*, and of course that is equivalent to a *command* for me to go to his house."

I assured her that she might make her mind at ease, for whatever might be the custom with crowned heads, our Presidents were not wont to "command" the movements of strangers, and that she would be quite in time if she returned his call the next day. She did so, and was charmed with the unaffected bearing of the President, and the warm kindnesses expressed by his amiable wife and daughter, (now, alas! both tenants of the grave,) and consented to spend the evening with them in conformity with their request. She was accompanied to the "White House" by Messrs. Benedict, Belletti and myself, and several happy hours were spent in the private circle of the President's family. . . .

Both concerts in Washington were attended by the President and his family, and every member of the Cabinet. I noticed also among the audience, Messrs. Clay, Benton, Cass, General Scott, etc. On the following morning, she was called upon by Mr. Webster, Mr. Clay, General Cass, and Colonel Benton, and all parties were evidently gratified. I had introduced Mr. Webster to Jenny in Boston. Upon hearing one of her wild mountain songs in New-York, also in Washington, Mr. Webster signified his approval by rising, drawing himself up to his full height, and making a profound bow. Jenny was delighted by this expression of praise from the great statesman.

We visited the Capitol while both Houses were in session. Miss Lind took the arm of Hon. C. F. Cleveland, representative from Connecticut, and was by him escorted into various parts of the Capitol, the grounds, etc., with all of which she was much pleased.

While in Washington, I was invited with Miss Lind and her immediate friends to visit Mount Vernon, with Colonel Washington, the present proprietor, and Mr. Seaton, ex-Mayor of Washington, and Editor of the Intelligencer. Colonel Washington chartered a steamboat for the purpose. We were landed a short distance from the tomb, which we first visited. Proceeding to the house, we were introduced to Mrs. Washington and several other ladies. Much interest was manifested by Miss Lind in examining the mementoes of the great man whose home it had been. A beautiful collation was spread out and arranged in fine taste. Before leaving, Mrs. Washington presented Jenny with a book from the library, with the name of Washington written by his own hand. She was much overcome at receiving this present, called me aside, and expressed her desire to give something in return. "I have nothing with me," she said, "excepting this watch and chain, and I will give that if you think it will be acceptable." I knew the watch was very valuable, and told her that so costly a present would not be expected, nor would it be proper. "The expense is nothing, compared to the value of that book," she replied with deep emotion; "but as the watch was a present from a dear friend, perhaps I should not give it away." Jenny Lind, I am sure, will never forget the pleasurable emotions of that day. . . .

We reached New-York early in May, 1851, and gave fourteen concerts in Castle Garden and Metropolitan Hall. The last of these made the ninety-second regular concert under our engagement. Jenny had now again reached the atmosphere of her "advisers," and I soon discovered the effects of their influence. I, however, cared little what course they advised her to pursue. I indeed wished they would prevail upon her to close with her hundredth concert, for I had become weary with constant excitement and unremitting exertions. I was confident that if Jenny undertook to give concerts on her own account, she would be imposed upon and harassed in a thousand ways; yet I felt it would be well for her to have a trial at it, if she saw fit to credit their assurance that I had not managed the enterprise as successfully as it might have been done.

At about the eighty-fifth concert, therefore, I was most happy to learn from her lips that she had concluded to pay the forfeiture of twenty-five thousand dollars, and terminate the concerts with the one hundredth.

We went to Philadelphia, where I had advertised the ninety-second, ninety-third, and ninety-fourth concerts, and had engaged the large National Theatre in Chestnut street. It had been used for equestrian and theatrical entertainments, but was now thoroughly cleansed and fitted up by Max Maretzek for Italian Opera. It was a convenient place for our purpose. One of her "advisers," a subordinate in her employ, who was already itching for the position of manager, made the selection of this building a pretext for causing dissatisfaction in the mind of Miss Lind. I saw the influences which were at work, and not caring enough for the profits of the remaining seven concerts to continue the engagement at the risk of disturbing the friendly feelings which had hitherto uninterruptedly existed between that lady and myself, I wrote her a letter offering to relinquish the engagement, if she desired it, at the termination of the concert which was to take place that evening, upon her simply allowing me a thousand dollars per concert for the seven which would yet remain to make up the hundred, besides paying me the sum stipulated as a forfeiture for closing the engagement at the one hundredth concert. Towards evening I received the following reply:

"To P. T. Barnum, Esq.

"My Dear Sir:—I accept your proposition to close our contract to-night, at the end of the ninety-third concert, on condition of my paying you seven thousand dollars in addition to the sum I forfeit under the condition of finishing the engagment at the end of one hundred concerts.

"I am, dear Sir, yours truly,
Jennt Lind.

"*Philadelphia*, 9th of June, 1851."

. . . Jenny gave several concerts with varied success, and then retired to Niagara Falls, and afterwards to Northampton, Mass. While sojourning at the latter place, she visited Boston and was married to Mr. Otto Goldschmidt, a German composer and pianist, to whom she was much attached, and who had studied music with her in Germany. He played several times in our concerts. He seemed a very quiet, inoffensive gentleman, is an accomplished musician, and I have no doubt he makes Miss Lind a good husband.

I met her several times after our engagement terminated. She was always affable. On one occasion, while passing through Bridgeport, she told me that she had been sadly harassed in giving her concerts. "People cheat me and swindle me very much," said she, "and I find it very annoying to give concerts on my own account."

I was always supplied with tickets when she gave concerts in New-York, and on the occasion of her last appearance in America, I visited her in her room back of the stage, and bade herself and husband adieu, with my best wishes. She expressed the same feeling to me in return. She told me she should never sing much if any more in public, but I begged her, for the public's sake, not to retire altogether; to which she replied, that she might occasionally give some concerts. I believe nothing would induce her again to appear in opera.

After so many months of anxiety, labor and excitement, in the Jenny Lind enterprise, it will readily be believed that I desired tranquillity. I spent a week at Cape May, and then "came home" to Iranistan, where I remained the entire summer.

XII. "SIDE SHOWS"—BUFFALO HUNT, ETC.

In attending to what might be termed my "side shows," or temporary enterprises, I have never neglected the American Museum. This was my first really successful effort in life, and I have constantly endeavored to increase its attractions, regardless of expense.

While in Europe, I was constantly on the look-out for novelties. Not a fair was held, within a reasonable distance, that I did not visit, with a view to buy or hire such exhibitions as I thought would "pay" in the United States. . . .

In 1849, I projected a great travelling museum and menagerie. Having neither time nor inclination to manage such a concern, I induced Mr. Seth B. Howes, justly celebrated as "a showman," join me, and take the sole charge. Mr. Sherwood E. Stratton, father of General Tom Thumb, was also introduced, the interest being in thirds.

In carrying out a portion of the plan, we chartered the ship "Regatta," Captain Pratt, and dispatched her, together with our agents, Messrs. June and Nutter, to Ceylon. The ship left New-York in May, 1850, and was absent one year. Their mission was to procure, either by capture or purchase, twelve or more living elephants, besides such other wild animals as they could secure. In order to provide sufficient drink and provender for a cargo of these huge animals, we purchased a large quantity of hay in New-York. Five hundred tons of it was left at the island of St. Helena, to be taken on the return trip of the ship. Staves and hoops of water-casks were also left at St. Helena.

Our agents, being unable to purchase the required number of elephants, either in Columbo or Kandy, the principal towns of the island,

(Ceylon,) took one hundred and sixty native assistants, and plunged into the jungles, where, after many most exciting adventures, they succeeded in securing thirteen elephants of a suitable size for their purpose, with a female and her calf, or "baby" elephant, only six months old. In the course of the expedition, Messrs. Nutter and June killed large numbers of the huge beasts, and had numerous encounters of the most terrific description with the formidable animals, one of the most fearful of which took place on the 23d November, 1850, near Anarajah Poora, while endeavoring by the aid of the natives and trained elephants to drive the wild herd of beasts into an Indian kraal.

They arrived in New-York with ten of the elephants, and also brought with them one of the natives who was competent to their management. We added a caravan of wild animals and many museum curiosities — the entire outfit, including horses, vans, carriages, tent, etc., costing $109,000 — and commenced operations, with the presence and under the patronage of Gen. Tom Thumb! who has now travelled four years as one of the attractions of "Barnum's great Asiatic Caravan, Museum, and Menagerie."

The popularity of this exhibition attracted numerous "side-shows" by other parties, greatly to our annoyance. In self-defence we fitted out a circus company, which performs on the same day and in the same neighborhood that the menagerie and museum are exhibited. Should an opposition threaten interference with us, we need only connect our two companies at the single price of admission, and competition is impossible. Our receipts in four years reached nearly one million dollars.

It will be admitted that these enterprises are legitimate, though I have been engaged in several which have been considered doubtful. It is not my business to dispute the point, but to narrate the facts — as follows:

The Woolly Horse. — In the summer of 1848, while in Cincinnati with General Tom Thumb, my attention was arrested by handbills announcing the exhibition of a "woolly horse." Being always on the *qui vive*[32] for every thing curious with which to amuse or astonish the public, I visited the exhibition, and found the animal to be a veritable curiosity. It was a well-formed horse of rather small size, without any mane or the slightest portion of hair upon his tail. The entire body and limbs were covered with a thick fine hair or wool curling tight to his skin. He was foaled in Indiana, was a mere freak of nature, and withal a very curious-looking animal. I purchased him and sent him to Bridgeport, Ct., where he was placed quietly away in a retired barn, until such time as I might have use for him.

[32]Meaning "on the lookout."

The occasion at last occurred. Col. Fremont was lost among the trackless snows of the Rocky Mountains. The public mind was excited. Serious apprehensions existed that the intrepid soldier and engineer had fallen a victim to the rigors of a severe winter. At last the mail brought intelligence of his safety. The public heart beat quick with joy. I now saw a chance for the "woolly horse." He was carefully covered with blankets and leggings, so that nothing could be seen excepting his eyes and hoofs, conveyed to New-York, and deposited in a rear stable, where no eye of curiosity could reach him.

The next mail was said to have brought intelligence that Col. Fremont and his hardy band of warriors had, after a three days chase, succeeded in capturing, near the river Gila, a most extraordinary nondescript, which somewhat resembled a horse, but which had no mane nor tail, and was covered with a thick coat of wool. The account further added that the Colonel had sent this wonderful animal as a present to the U. S. Quarter-master.

Two days after this announcement, the following advertisement appeared in the New-York papers:

> "Col. Fremont's Nondescript or Woolly Horse will be exhibited for a few days at the corner of Broadway and Reade street, previous to his departure for London. Nature seems to have exerted all her ingenuity in the production of this astounding animal. He is extremely complex — made up of the Elephant, Deer, Horse, Buffalo, Camel, and Sheep. It is the full size of a Horse, has the haunches of the Deer, the tail of the Elephant, a fine curled wool of camel's hair color, and easily bounds twelve or fifteen feet high. Naturalists and the oldest trappers assured Col. Fremont that it was never known previous to his discovery. It is undoubtedly 'Nature's last,' and the richest specimen received from California. To be seen every day this week. Admittance 25 cents; children half price."

The building where he was exhibited, exactly opposite Stuart's immense dry-goods store, was mounted by several large transparencies representing the "Nondescript" in full flight, pursued by the brave Fremont and his hardy handful of soldiers. The streets were also lined with handbills and posters, illustrating in wood-cuts the same thrilling event. . . .

But the public appetite was craving something tangible from Col. Fremont. The community was absolutely famishing. They were ravenous. They could have swallowed any thing, and like a good genius, I threw them, not a "bone," but a regular tit-bit, a bon-bon—and they swallowed it at a single gulp!

My agent tried "Old Woolly" in several of the provincial towns with tolerable success, and finally he was taken to Washington city, to see if the wool could be pulled over the eyes of politicians. It was successfully done for several days, when Col. Benton,[33] ever regardful of the reputation of his son-in-law, caused my agent to be arrested on a grand-jury complaint for obtaining from him twenty-five cents under false pretences, and the Senator from Missouri testified, that having no mention of this horse in any of the numerous letters received from his son-in-law, he was sure Col. Fremont never saw the animal.

Such testimony could not prove a negative. The complaint was ruled out, and "Old Woolly" came off victorious. The excitement which Col. Benton unconsciously produced added materially to the receipts for the succeeding few days. But, always entertaining the greatest respect for "Old Bullion," and out of regard to his feelings, I ordered the horse back to Bridgeport, where in due time he gave his last kick.

For some time, however, he was turned loose in a field lying on the public road, where occasional New-York patrons recognized their woolly friend in his retirement.

The Buffalo Hunt.—I attended the great Bunker Hill celebration, June 17, 1843, and heard Mr. Webster's oration. I found exhibiting near the monument, under an old canvas tent, a herd of calf buffaloes a year old. There were fifteen in number, and I purchased the lot for $700. I had an idea in my head which, if I could carry it out, would make the buffaloes a profitable investment, and I was determined to try it. The animals were poor and remarkably docile, having been driven from the plains of the Great West. I had them brought to New-York, and placed in a farmer's barn in New-Jersey, near Hoboken. Mr. C. D. French, of whom I purchased them, understood throwing the *lasso*, and I hired him for $30 per month to take care of the buffaloes, until such time as I had matured my plans.

Paragraphs were soon started in the papers announcing that a herd of wild buffaloes, caught by the lasso when quite young, were now on their way from the Rocky Mountains to Europe, *via* New-York, in charge of the men who captured them. In a few days communications appeared in several papers, suggesting that if the buffaloes could be safely secured in some race course, and a regular buffalo chase given by their owners, showing the use of the *lasso*, etc., it would be a treat worth going many

---

[33]Thomas Hart Benton—known as "Old Bullion"—was a prominent senator from Missouri. His daughter, Jessie Ann Benton, had married John C. Frémont in 1841.

miles to see. One correspondent declared it would be worth a dollar to see it; another asserted that fifty thousand persons would gladly pay to witness it, etc. One suggested the Long Island Race Course; another thought a large plot of ground at Harlem, inclosed expressly for the purpose, would be better; and a third suggested Hoboken as just the place. In due time, the following advertisement appeared in the public prints, and handbills and posters of the same purport, illustrated by the following picture of wild buffaloes pursued by Indians on horseback, were simultaneously circulated, far and near, with a liberal hand:

"Grand Buffalo Hunt, Free of Charge.—At Hoboken, on Thursday, August 31, at 3, 4, and 5 o'clock P. M. Mr. C. D. French, one of the most daring and experienced hunters of the West, has arrived thus far on his way to Europe, with a Herd of Buffaloes, captured by himself, near Santa Fé. He will exhibit the method of hunting the Wild Buffaloes, and throwing the lasso, by which the animals were captured in their most wild and untamed state. This is perhaps one of the most exciting and difficult feats that can be performed, requiring at the same time the most expert horsemanship and the greatest skill and dexterity. . . .

"No possible danger need be apprehended, as a double railing has been put around the whole course, to prevent the possibility of the Buffaloes approaching the multitude. Extra ferry-boats will be provided, to run from Barclay, Canal, and Christopher streets. . . .

The mystery of a free exhibition of the sort, though not understood at the time, is readily explained. I had engaged all the ferry boats to Hoboken, at a stipulated price, and all the receipts on the day specified were to be mine.

The assurance that no danger need be apprehended from the buffaloes was simply ridiculous. The poor creatures were so weak and tame that it was doubtful whether they would run at all, notwithstanding my man French had been cramming them with oats to get a little extra life into them.

The eventful day arrived. Taking time by the forelock, multitudes of people crossed to Hoboken before ten o'clock, and by noon the ferry-boats were constantly crowded to their utmost capacity. An extra boat, the Passaic, was put on, and the rush of passengers continued until five o'clock. Twenty-four thousand persons went by the ferry-boats to Hoboken that day. Each paid six and a quarter cents going, and as much returning, and the aggregate receipts, including the ferriage of carts and carriages, and the hire for refreshment-stands on the ground, were $3500. Many thousand persons were present from various parts of New-Jersey, and these, though bringing "grist to my mill," of course escaped my "toll" at the ferries.

The band of music engaged for the occasion, did its best to amuse the immense crowd until three o'clock. At precisely that hour the buffaloes emerged from a shed in the centre of the inclosure—my man French having previously administered a punching with a sharp stick, hoping to excite them to a trot on their first appearance. He immediately followed them, painted and dressed as an Indian, mounted on a fiery steed, with lasso in one hand and a sharp stick in the other, but the poor little calves huddled together, and refused to move! This scene was so wholly unexpected, and so perfectly ludicrous, that the spectators burst into uncontrollable uproarious laughter. The shouting somewhat startled the buffaloes, and, goaded by French and his assistants, they started off in a slow trot. The uproar of merriment was renewed, and the multitude swinging their hats and hallooing in wild disorder, the buffaloes broke into a gallop, ran against a panel of the low fence, (consisting of two narrow boards,) tumbled over, and scrambled away as fast as they could. The crowd in that quarter offered no obstruction. Seeing the animals approach, and not being sufficiently near to discover how harmless they were, men, women and children scattered pell-mell! Such a scampering I never saw before. The buffaloes, which were as badly frightened as the people, found shelter in a neighboring swamp, and all efforts to disengage them proved ineffectual. French, however, captured one of them with his lasso, and afterwards amused the people by lassoing horses and riders—and good-humor prevailed.

No one seemed to suspect the ferry-boat arrangement—the projector was *incog.*—the exhibition had been free to the public—there had been much amusement for twelve and a half cents each, and no one complained. It was, however, nearly midnight before all the visitors found ferry accommodations to New-York.

N. P. Willis, of the "Home Journal," wrote an article illustrating the perfect good-nature with which the American public submits to a clever humbug. He said that he went to Hoboken to witness the Buffalo Hunt. It was nearly four o'clock when the boat left the foot of Barclay street, yet it was so densely crowded that many persons were obliged to stand upon the railings and hold on to the awning posts. When they reached the Hoboken side, a boat equally crowded was leaving that wharf. The passengers of the boat just arriving cried out to those in the boat just returning, "Is the Buffalo Hunt over?" To which came the reply, "Yes, and it was the biggest humbug you ever heard of!" Willis added, that the passengers on the boat with him were so delighted, that they instantly gave three cheers for the author of the humbug, whoever he might be. . . .

XIII. TEMPERANCE AND AGRICULTURE

In the fall of 1847, while exhibiting Gen. Tom Thumb at Saratoga Springs, where the New-York State Fair was then being held, I saw so much intoxication among men of wealth and intellect, filling the highest positions in society, that I began to ask myself the question, What guarantee is there that *I* may not become a drunkard? I reflected that many wiser and better men than myself had fallen victims to intemperance; and although I was not in the habit of partaking often of strong drink, I was liable to do so whenever I met friends, which in my travels occurred every day. Hence I resolved to fly the danger, and I pledged myself at that time never again to partake of any kind of spirituous liquors as a beverage.

I now felt that I was out of danger, and the sensation was a pleasant one. True, I continued to partake of wine, for I had been instructed, in my European tour, that this was one of the innocent and charming indispensables of life. I however regarded myself as a good temperance man, and soon began to persuade my friends to refrain from the intoxicating cup. Seeing need of reform in Bridgeport, I invited my friend the Rev. E. H. Chapin to visit us, for the purpose of giving a public temperance lecture. I had never heard him on that subject, but I knew that on whatever topic he spoke, he was as logical as eloquent.

He lectured in the Baptist Church in Bridgeport. His subject was presented in three divisions: The liquor-seller, the moderate drinker, and the indifferent man. It happened, therefore, that the second, if not the third clause of the subject, had a special bearing upon *me* and my position.

The eloquent gentleman overwhelmingly proved that the so–called respectable liquor-seller, in his splendid saloon or hotel bar, and who sold only to "gentlemen," inflicted much greater injury upon the community than a dozen common groggeries—which he abundantly illustrated.

He then took up the "moderate drinker," and urged that *he* was the great stumbling-block to the temperance reform. He it was, and not the drunkard in the ditch, that the young man looked at as an example when he took his first glass. That when the drunkard was asked to sign the pledge, he would reply, "Why should I do so? What harm can there be in drinking, when such men as respectable Mr. A, and moral Mr. B, drink wine under their own roof?" He urged that the higher a man stood in the community, the greater was his influence either for good or for evil. He said to the moderate drinker: "Sir, you either do or you do not consider it a privation and a sacrifice to give up drinking. Which is it? If you say that you can drink or let it alone, that you can quit it for ever without considering it a self-denial, then I appeal to you as a man, to do it for *the sake of your suffering fellow-beings.* If, on the other hand, you say that you like to indulge moderately in the use of intoxicating drinks, and that it would be a self denial on your part to abandon the practice, then, sir, I warn you in the light of all human experience, that you are *in danger*, and should give it up *for your own sake.* When appetite has so far got its hold upon you as to make the thought of abandoning strong drink uncomfortable, I tell you that the chances are strongly in favor of your dying a drunkard, unless you renounce the use of intoxicating beverages altogether."

I do not pretend to give the precise language of the eloquent Mr. Chapin, and no man can depict the overwhelming power with which he urged his position. But I have given the gist of his argument as applied to the moderate drinker. It sank most deeply into my heart. I returned home and went to bed, but not to sleep. These arguments continued to ring in my ears, and though striving to find a reasonable answer to them, I spent a wretched and sleepless night. I had become fully conscious that I was pursuing a path of wrong-doing, and one which was not only causing great wrong to the community, but also fraught with imminent danger to myself.

I arose from my bed, and feeling that as a man I could not persist in a practice which I could not conscientiously and logically defend, I took my champagne bottles, knocked off their heads, and poured their contents upon the ground. I then called upon Mr. Chapin, asked him for the teetotal pledge,[34] and signed it.

God knows I am determined never to break that pledge, and my gratitude is so deep at being thus placed in a position to benefit my fellow-man, as well as perhaps to save myself, that I trust there is little danger of my ever again being brought within the charmed circle of the cup. Upon informing my wife that I had signed the teetotal pledge, I was surprised to see tears running down her cheeks. I was afterwards astonished to know from her, that she had passed many a weeping night, fearing that my wine-bibbing was leading me to a drunkard's path. I reproached her for not telling me her fears, but she replied that she

---

[34]Abstinence from alcohol.

knew I was self deluded, and that any such hint from her would have been received in anger.

This, let me here observe, is the case of thousands of individuals to-day. They are moving in respectable society, and regard intemperance as a dreadful evil. They would despise the thought of ever becoming intemperate themselves, and would look upon such a suggestion as the height of impudence and folly. The man who commences tippling is the last person in the world to discover his danger. If he has a wife, she probably is the first to know and shudder at his position. His neighbors know it long before he is aware of it, and if instead of passing it by in silence, as is usually the case, they would candidly point out to him the perilous course he is pursuing, many a valuable member of society would be saved from degradation, and his happy family snatched from misery, disgrace and despair.

I thanked Mr. Chapin, from my heart of hearts, for being the instrument of saving me, and great was his astonishment in discovering that I was not already a teetotaller. He supposed such was the case from the fact that I had invited him to lecture, and he little thought, at the time of his delivering it, that his argument to the moderate drinker was at all applicable to me. But it was, and through the mercy of God, it saved me.

I now felt that I had a great duty to perform. I had been groping in darkness, was rescued, and I knew it was my duty to try and save others. The morning that I signed the pledge, I obtained over twenty signatures in Bridgeport. I talked temperance to all whom I met, and very soon commenced lecturing upon the subject in the adjacent towns and villages. I spent the entire winter and spring of 1851–2 in lecturing through my native State, always travelling at my own expense, and I was glad to know that I aroused many hundreds, perhaps thousands, to the importance of the temperance reform. I also lectured frequently in the cities of New-York and Philadelphia, as well as in other towns in the neighboring States.

About this time the Maine Law[35] was enacted, and its successful workings filled the hearts of temperance men and temperance women with hope and joy. We soon learned that in order to stay the plague, we must have a total prohibition of the sale of intoxicating drinks as a beverage. Neal Dow[36] (may God bless him!) had opened our eyes. We saw that moral suasion had done much good. We could see that

---

[35]In 1851, Maine became the first state in the nation to ban the sale of alcohol.
[36]Neal Dow, the mayor of Portland, Maine, had been a driving force behind the law's passage.

the Washingtonians and Sons of Temperance, the Daughters of Temperance, the Rechabites, and the Temples of Honor,[37] had discharged their mission of peace and love; but we also saw that large numbers who were saved by these means, fell back again to a lower position than ever, because the tempter was permitted to live and throw out his seductive toils.

Our watchword now was, "Prohibition!" We had become convinced that it was a matter of life and death; that we must *kill* Alcohol, or Alcohol would kill *us*, or our friends.

While in Boston with Jenny Lind, I was earnestly solicited to deliver two temperance lectures in the Tremont Temple, where she gave her concerts. I did so, and although an admission of twelve and a half cents was charged for the benefit of a benevolent society, the building on each occasion was crowded.

In the course of my tour with Jenny Lind, I was frequently solicited to lecture on temperance on evenings when she did not sing. I always complied when it was in my power. In this way I lectured in Baltimore, Washington, Charleston, New-Orleans, St. Louis, Cincinnati, etc—also in the ladies' saloon of the steamer Lexington, on Sabbath morning.

In August, 1853, I lectured in Cleveland, Ohio, and several other towns, and afterwards in Chicago, Illinois, and in Kenosha, Wisconsin. In the latter State I found the field was nearly ready for the harvest, but there were few reapers. A State election was to come off in October, on which occasion the people were to decide by ballot whether they would or would not approve of a prohibitory liquor law. Owing to an immense German population, who in the main were opposed to prohibition, the temperance friends were apprehensive of the result. They solicited my services for the ensuing month. I could not refuse them. I therefore hastened home to transact some business which required my presence for a few days, and then returned, and lectured on my way in Toledo and Norwalk, Ohio, and Chicago, Illinois. I made the tour of the State of Wisconsin, delivering two lectures per day for four consecutive weeks, to crowded and attentive audiences. I was glad to believe that my efforts contributed to a good result. The voice of the people declared, by a wholesome majority, in favor of a prohibitory liquor law, but a political legislature, hostile to so beneficent an act, refused to give it to them. I trust their deliverance is not far off. . . .

---

[37]Washingtonians, the Sons of Temperance, the Daughters of Temperance, the Rechabites, and the Temples of Honor were all names of different temperance groups active in the United States and Great Britain at this time.

Among the most gratifying incidents of my life, have been several of a similar nature to the following:

After a temperance speech in Philadelphia, a man about thirty years of age came forward, signed the teetotal pledge, and then, giving me his hand, he said, "Mr. Barnum, you have this night saved me from ruin. For the last two years I have been in the habit of tippling, and it has kept me continually under the harrow. This gentleman (pointing to a person at his side) is my partner in business, and I know he is glad I have signed the pledge to-night."

"Yes, indeed I am, George, and it is the best thing you ever did," replied his partner, " if you'll only stick to it"

"That will I do till the day of my death; and won't my dear little wife Mary cry for joy to-night when I tell her what I have done!" he exclaimed in great exultation.

At that moment he was a happy man—but he could not have been more so than I was. . . .

XIV. SUNDRY BUSINESS ENTERPRISES

. . . In 1852, Edwin T. Freedley Esq., of Philadelphia, informed me by letter that he was about to publish a book, entitled a "Practical Treatise on Business," and he desired me to furnish him a communication embodying *the results* of my experience and observation. I wrote him the following article, which he published in his valuable work under the title.

BARNUM'S RULES FOR SUCCESS IN BUSINESS

1. *Select the kind of business that suits your natural inclinations and temperament.* Some men are naturally mechanics; others have a strong aversion to any thing like machinery, and so on; one man has a natural taste for one occupation, and another for another. . . .

   I never could succeed as a merchant. I have tried it unsuccessfully several times. I never could be content with a fixed salary, for mine is a purely speculative disposition, while others are just the reverse; and therefore all should be careful to select those occupations that suit them best.

2. *Let your pledged word ever be sacred.* Never promise to do a thing without performing it with the most rigid promptness. Nothing is more valuable to a man in business than the name of always doing as he agrees, and that to the moment. A strict adherence to this rule,

gives a man the command of half the spare funds within the range of his acquaintance, and always encircles him with a host of friends who may be depended upon in almost any conceivable emergency.

3. *Whatever you do, do with all your might.* Work at it if necessary early and late, in season and out of season, not leaving a stone unturned, and never deferring for a single hour that which can be done just as well *now.* The old proverb is full of truth and meaning, "Whatever is worth doing at all, is worth doing well." Many a man acquires a fortune by doing his business *thoroughly* while his neighbor remains poor for life because he only *half* does his business. Ambition, energy, industry, perseverance, are indispensable requisites for success in business.

4. *Sobriety. Use no description of intoxicating drinks.* As no man can succeed in business unless he has a *brain* to enable him to lay his plans, and *reason* to guide him in their execution, so, no matter how bountifully a man may be blessed with intelligence, if his brain is muddled, and his judgment warped by intoxicating drinks, it is impossible for him to carry on business successfully. How many good opportunities have passed never to return, while a man was sipping a "social glass" with his friend! How many foolish bargains have been made under the influence of *nervine* [a medication or tonic used to calm anxiety or nervousness or otherwise aid the nervous system], which temporarily makes its victim so *rich*! How many important chances have been put off until to-morrow, and thence for ever, because the wine-cup has thrown the system into a state of lassitude, neutralizing the energies so essential to success in business. The use of intoxicating drinks as a beverage is as much an infatuation as is the smoking of opium by the Chinese, and the former is quite as destructive to the success of the business man as the latter.

5. *Let hope predominate, but be not too visionary.* Many persons are always kept poor, because they are too *visionary.* Every project looks to them like certain success, and therefore they keep changing from one business to another, always in hot water, always "under the harrow." The plan of "counting the chickens before they are hatched" is an error of ancient date, but it does not seem to improve by age.

6. *Do not scatter your powers.* Engage in one kind of business only, and stick to it faithfully until you succeed, or until you conclude to abandon it. A constant hammering on one nail, will generally drive it home at last, so that it can be clinched. When a man's undivided

attention is centred on one object, his mind will constantly be suggesting improvements of value, which would escape him if his brain were occupied by a dozen different subjects at once. Many a fortune has slipped through men's fingers by engaging in too many occupations at once.

7. *Engage proper employees.* Never employ a man of bad habits, when one whose habits are good can be found to fill his situation. I have generally been extremely fortunate in having faithful and competent persons to fill the responsible situations in my business, and a man can scarcely be too grateful for such a blessing. When you find a man unfit to fill his station, either from incapacity or peculiarity of character or disposition, dispense with his services, and do not drag out a miserable existence in the vain attempt to change his nature. It is utterly impossible to do so. "You cannot make a silk purse," etc. He was created for some other sphere. Let him find and fill it.

8. *Advertise your business. Do not hide your light under a bushel.* Whatever your occupation or calling may be, if it needs support from the public, *advertise* it thoroughly and efficiently, in some shape or other, that will arrest public attention. I freely confess that what success I have had in my life may fairly be attributed more to the public press than to nearly all other causes combined. There *may* possibly be occupations that do not require advertising, but I cannot well conceive what they are.

Men in business will sometimes tell you that they have tried advertising, and that it did not pay. This is only when advertising is done sparingly and grudgingly. Homoeopathic[38] doses of advertising will not pay perhaps—it is like half a potion of physic, making the patient sick, but effecting nothing. Administer liberally, and the cure will be sure and permanent.

Some say, "they cannot afford to advertise;" they mistake— they cannot afford *not* to advertise. In this country, where everybody reads the newspapers, the man must have a thick skull who does not see that these are the cheapest and best medium through which he can speak to the public, where he is to find his customers. Put on the *appearance* of business, and generally the *reality* will follow. The farmer plants his seed, and while he is sleeping, his corn and potatoes are growing. So with advertising.

---

[38]A system of medicine that attempts to cure the sick by administering minute doses of substances that would, in a full dose, make a healthy person sick.

While you are sleeping, or eating, or conversing with one set of customers, your advertisement is being read by hundreds and thousands of persons who never saw you, nor heard of your business, and never would, had it not been for your advertisement appearing in the newspapers.

The business men of this country do not, as a general thing, appreciate the advantages of advertising thoroughly. Occasionally the public are aroused at witnessing the succcess of a Swaim, a Brandreth, a Townsend, a Genin, or a Root,[39] and express astonishment at the rapidity with which these gentlemen acquire fortunes, not reflecting that the same path is open to all who *dare* pursue it. But it needs *nerve* and *faith*. The former, to enable you to launch out thousands on the uncertain waters of the future; the latter, to teach you that after many days it shall surely return, bringing an hundred or a thousand fold to him who appreciates the advantages of "printer's ink" properly applied.

9. *Avoid extravagance; and always live considerably within your income, if you can do so without absolute starvation!* It needs no prophet to tell us that those who live fully up to their means, without any thought of a reverse in life, can never attain to a pecuniary independence.

Men and women accustomed to gratify every whim and caprice will find it hard at first to cut down their various unnecessary expenses, and will feel it a great self-denial to live in a smaller house than they have been accustomed to, with less expensive furniture, less company, less costly clothing, a less number of balls, parties, theatre-goings, carriage ridings, pleasure excursions, cigar smokings, liquor-drinkings, etc., etc., etc.; but, after all, if they will try the plan of laying by a "nest-egg," or in other words, a small sum of money, after paying all expenses, they will be surprised at the pleasure to be derived from constantly adding to their little "pile," as well as from all the economical habits which follow in the pursuit of this peculiar pleasure.

The old suit of clothes, and the old bonnet and dress, will answer for another season; the Croton[40] or spring water will taste better than champagne; a brisk walk will prove more exhilarating than a ride in the finest coach; a social family chat, an evening's

---

[39]Barnum is here listing a number of contemporary entrepreneurs who built fortunes very quickly. Several of them — William Swaim, Benjamin Brandreth, and S. P. Townsend — amassed their riches by selling quack remedies and panaceas.

[40]Water piped into New York City via the Croton Aqueduct.

reading in the family circle, or an hour's play of "hunt the slipper" and "blind man's buff," will be far more pleasant than a fifty, or a five hundred dollar party, when the reflection on the *difference in cost* is indulged in by those who begin to know the *pleasures of saving*.

Thousands of men are kept poor, and tens of thousands are made so after they have acquired quite sufficient to support them well through life, in consequence of laying their plans of living on too expensive a platform. Some families in this country expend twenty thousand dollars per annum, and some much more, and would scarcely know how to live on a less sum.

Prosperity is a more severe ordeal than adversity, especially sudden prosperity. "Easy come, easy go," is an old and true proverb. *Pride*, when permitted full sway, is the great undying cankerworm which gnaws the very vitals of a man's worldly possessions, let them be small or great, hundreds or millions. Many persons, as they begin to prosper, immediately commence expending for luxuries, until in a short time their expenses swallow up their income, and they become ruined in their ridiculous attempts to keep up appearances, and make a "sensation."

I know a gentleman of fortune, who says, that when he first began to prosper, his wife *would have* a new and elegant sofa "That sofa," he says, "cost me thirty thousand dollars!" The riddle is thus explained:

When the sofa reached the house, it was found necessary to get chairs to "match," then sideboards, carpets and tables, "to correspond" with them, and so on through the entire stock of furniture, when at last it was found that the house itself was quite too small and old-fashioned for the furniture, and a new one was built to correspond with the sofa and *et ceteras*; "thus," added my friend, "running up an outlay of thirty thousand dollars caused by that single sofa, and saddling on me, in the shape of servants, equipage, and the necessary expenses attendant upon keeping up a fine 'establishment,' a yearly outlay of eleven thousand dollars, and a tight pinch at that; whereas, ten years ago, we lived with much more real comfort, because with much less care, on as many hundreds. The truth is," he continued, "that sofa would have brought me to inevitable bankruptcy, had not a most unexampled tide of prosperity kept me above it."

10. *Do not depend upon others.* Your success must depend upon your own individual exertions. Trust not to the assistance of

friends; but learn that every man must be the architect of his own fortune.

With proper attention to the foregoing rules, and such observations as a man of sense will pick up in his own experience, the road to competence will not, I think, usually be found a difficult one.

P. T. Barnum.

In taking a survey of the chequered career which is described in these pages, I shall perhaps disagree with some of my more straight-laced but very worthy readers as to the value and significance of that career, and as to the degree of consideration which it shows that I have justly earned from the public. I shall however give my candid opinion upon the subject, even at the risk of being charged with egotism.

The great defect in our American civilization, it is generally acknowledged by observing and thoughtful men, is a severe and drudging practicalness—a practicalness which is not commendable, because it loses sight of the true aims of life, and concentrates itself upon dry and technical ideas of duty, and upon a sordid love of acquisition—leaving entirely out of view all those needful and proper relaxations and enjoyments which are interwoven through even the most humble conditions in other countries. If in the Catholic states of Europe there are too many holidays, with us the fault is on the other side: we have none at all. The consequence is, that with the most universal diffusion of the means of happiness ever known among any people, we are unhappy. Without ideality, "a primrose by the river's brim" does not arrest the attention of the American; the flower "a simple primrose is to him, and it is nothing more."

With their traditions and habits, our countrymen, of the middling classes, inherit in too great a degree a capacity only for the most valueless and irrational enjoyments, and their inclination to intemperance and kindred vices has repeatedly and most conclusively been shown to be a natural result of the lamentable deficiency among us of innocent and rational amusements. I am not going to set up as a philosopher, but the venerable and illustrious name of Channing[41]—eminent alike for wisdom, benevolence, piety, and purity, for a private and public character unsurpassed in its elevation—may be adduced as earnestly and unqualifiedly supporting these views; and no higher authority, I conceive, has ever existed in this country upon morals and society, and especially upon the difficult subject which he illustrated so admirably in

---

[41]William Ellery Channing, a prominent Unitarian theologian of the era.

the noblest production of his genius, the essay "On the Elevation of the Laboring Portion of the Community."[42]

As a business man, undoubtedly, my prime object has been to put money in my purse. I succeeded beyond my most sanguine anticipations, and am satisfied. But what I have here said, will prepare the reader for what I conceive to be a just and altogether reasonable claim, that I have been a public benefactor, to an extent seldom paralleled in the histories of professed and professional philanthropists.

My travelling museums of natural history have been the largest and most interesting ever exhibited in the United States, and no author, or university even, has ever accomplished as much in the diffusion of a knowledge of the varied forms and classes of animal life. These, with my museums in New-York, Philadelphia, and Baltimore, have been one of the chief means by which I have instructed the masses.

For the elevation and refinement of musical taste in this country, it will not be denied that I have done more than any man living. By bringing Jenny Lind to the United States, I inaugurated a new era in the most beautiful and humanizing of all the fine arts, and gave to the cultivated and wealthy as well as to the middling classes a larger measure of enjoyment than has ever been derived from the enterprise of any other single individual.

I will not enter into a further recapitulation of the benefits I have conferred on my countrymen and countrywomen, as a minister to their instruction and happiness, while pursuing my main purpose of making money. The charges with which my claims in this respect will be met, are, simply, that I have *managed*, while my vocation has been that of a manager. It is granted. I have advertised my curiosities and my artists with all the ingenuity of which I was capable. My interests demanded that course, and it was my business to consult my interests in all legitimate ways. No one, however, for himself, can say that he ever paid for admission to one of my exhibitions more than his admission was worth to him. If a sight of my "Niagara Falls" was not worth twenty-five cents, the privilege of seeing the most extensive and valuable museum on this continent was worth double that sum to any one who was enticed into it by the advertisements of that ingenious contrivance. And I should like to see the moralist or the Christian who thinks my patron would have done as well with his money at the drinking den or any of the alternative places of buying entertainment.

---

[42]Though Channing supported child labor laws and other reforms, in this essay he urged working-class men and women to be content with their station in life, eschewing upward mobility and political power. Channing instead counseled workers to pursue the "elevation of their soul."

I might here close this book, hoping that the interest of some portions of it may be an offset to the dullness of others; but I must please myself, and perhaps gratify curiosity, by adding a brief history of my present residence, known as

IRANISTAN.

Finding, In 1846, that fortune continued to smile upon me, I began to look forward to the time when I could withdraw from the whirlpool of excitement, and permanently settle down with my family, to spend the remainder of my life in comparative tranquillity.

I wished to reside within a few hours of New-York. I never saw more delightful locations than upon the borders of Long Island Sound, between New-Rochelle, N.Y., and New-Haven, Conn.; and my attention was therefore turned in that direction. Bridgeport seemed to be about the proper distance from the great metropolis. It is pleasantly situated at the terminus of two railroads, which traverse the fertile valleys of the Naugatuck and Housatonic rivers. The enterprise which characterized the city, seemed to mark it as destined to become the first in the State in size and opulence; and I was not long in deciding, with the concurrence of my wife, to fix our future residence in that vicinity.

For this purpose I purchased seventeen acres of land, less than a mile west of the centre of the city, and fronting with a good view upon the Sound. Although nominally in Bridgeport, my residence is in Fairfield, a few rods west of the Bridgeport line.

In deciding upon the kind of house to be erected, I determined, first and foremost, to consult convenience and comfort. I cared little for style, and my wife cared still less; but as we meant to have a good house, it might as well, at the same time, be unique. In this, I confess, I had "an eye to business," for I thought that a pile of buildings of a novel order might indirectly serve as an advertisement of my various enterprises.

Visiting Brighton, I was greatly pleased with the Pavilion erected by George IV. It was the only specimen of Oriental architecture in England, and had not been introduced into America. I concluded to adopt it, and engaged a London architect to furnish me a set of drawings in the style of the Pavilion, differing sufficiently to be adapted to the spot of ground selected for my homestead.

On my first return to the United States, I brought these drawings with me—engaged a competent architect and builder, and gave him instructions to proceed with the work, not "by the job" but "by the day," and to spare neither time nor expense in erecting a comfortable, convenient, and tasteful residence.

The whole was finally completed to my satisfaction. My family removed into the premises, and on the fourteenth of November, 1848, nearly one thousand invited guests, including the poor and the rich, helped us in the old-fashioned custom of "house-warming."

"When the name Iranistan was announced, a waggish New-York editor syllabled it, *I-ran-i-stan*, and gave as the interpretation that *I ran* a long time before *I* could *stan*'! More correctly, how ever, the name signifies "Eastern Country Place," or, more poetically, "Oriental Villa."

I have no desire to ascertain the entire cost. All I care to know is, that it suits me, which would be a small consideration with me, did it not also suit my family.

I have seldom mentioned my wife and children in these pages, yet they have always been dearer to me than all things else in the wide world; and, whether in poverty or in abundance, no place on earth has ever been so attractive to me as my home.

My children are all daughters. Caroline C., the eldest, was born May 27, 1833, and married Mr. David W. Thompson, October 19, 1852. The name of their only child is Frances Barnum Thompson, born December 27, 1858. They reside a few rods west of Iranistan. The officiating clergyman was my esteemed friend the Rev. M. Ballou, whose fine abilities are equalled only by the geniality of his spirit. He resided at the time in Bridgeport, but has since removed to Hartford. Helen M., my second daughter, was born April 18, 1840. Frances J., the third, was born May 1, 1842, and died April 11, 1844. Pauline T., the fourth, was born March 1, 1846. . . .

I have not yet wholly retired from business, though I desire hereafter to restrict my attention chiefly to the American Museum and my interests in Bridgeport. I am frequently in New-York, and occasionally in other great cities, yet I am never so happy as when I return to my "homestead." I am writing the closing pages of this Autobiography on the sixth anniversary of the "house-warming," and my heart is warm with gratitude. I am at home, in the bosom of my family; and "home" and "family" are the highest and most expressive symbols of the kingdom of heaven.

PART THREE

Related Documents

1

NEW YORK DAILY TIMES

The Lessons of Barnum's Life
December 16, 1854

After the publication of the Life of P. T. Barnum *late in 1854, American newspapers and magazines widely reviewed the book. This review, which appeared in the forerunner of today's* New York Times, *is typical of the kind of unease that Barnum's autobiography provoked. Moralists distressed over a larger decline in commercial ethics voiced particular concerns about the autobiography's influence on young and impressionable readers, much as this review does in its closing paragraphs.*

In this country, more perhaps than in any other, Success is regarded as the test of worth:—and Barnum is the embodiment and impersonation of success. From being poor and obscure, he has rapidly made himself very rich and very famous. As a natural consequence he is watched, admired and envied by hundreds of thousands who are as poor as he was, and who are anxious to be as rich as he is. Young men especially,—that vast army of our American youth just entering upon active life, and embracing more of intellect, of intelligence, of active energy and enterprise than can be found perhaps elsewhere in the world,—look to Barnum with eager wonder and emulation. How has his splendid success been achieved? To what qualities of character, or to what business faculties, is it due? Mr. Barnum has written his life in order to satisfy these interrogations. He has narrated step by step the history of his career,—pointing out, for the amusement of the curious and the instruction of the ambitious, the path by which he has risen from poverty to wealth, and from obscurity to conspicuous influence. Of course the book will be eagerly and widely read. It will produce a very marked effect upon the sentiments and the conduct of the great body of the youth of America. It will do much towards guiding their ambition,—shaping their plans and directing their career. What is the lesson it is likely to teach?

"The Lessons of Barnum's Life," *New York Daily Times*, December 16, 1854

The great fact which Mr. Barnum sets forth in this biography of himself, is that his success has been achieved,—his wealth acquired,—his reputation and consideration established, by the systematic, adroit and persevering plan of *obtaining money under false pretences from the public at large.* This is the beginning and the end of his enterprise, and the great secret of his success. He seems occasionally conscious of the fact, and seeks to cloak it under phrases and forms of speech. He calls it *humbug,*—and, under the seeming candor of confession, palliates it by a variety of apologies and explanations. We must take men as we find them:—human nature is full of weaknesses, of which it is our right to take advantage:—men like to be deceived, if it be so cleverly done as to seem amusing;—no wrong is done if they get what they consider an equivalent for their money:—these are some of the moral maxims and reflections which are brought forward to palliate and excuse the leading fact, that his wealth has been acquired by a complicated system of falsehood and fraud. Mr. Barnum does not deny that the representations which have made his schemes successful have been false and fraudulent;—his only effort was to make the public appear to have been an accomplice in his plans, instead of their victim.

Mr. Barnum's profession has been that of a *showman,*—a business that may be honestly pursued. But he takes special pains to proclaim the fact that he pursued it dishonestly. He never recognized the slightest obligation, in the prosecution of it, to tell the truth, or offer his exhibitions to the public upon their merits. He said that Tom Thumb was *eleven* years old, when he knew he was only *five.* He represented Joice Heth as having been the nurse of Washington, when he knew she had not. He proclaimed that the Fejee mermaid was the remains of an actual animal, when he knew that it was a base fabrication. He asserted that the Woolly Horse was captured by Col. Fremont in the Rocky Mountains, when he knew that there was not one syllable of truth in the assertion. In all these schemes, as well as in all the others in which he was engaged, Mr. Barnum coined and promulgated the most distinct and deliberate falsehoods, and solicited and received money from millions of individuals on the strength of them. This was the way in which his fortune has been acquired. Other men do the same thing on a small scale. They sell sand for sugar,—chicory for coffee,—counterfeit bills for good ones; they seldom get rich and more frequently get into the State Prison. But this is not the fault of the *principle* of their action; but only of the mode in which it is carried out. They do not act upon a shrewd knowledge of human nature. They do not enlist the weaknesses of their victims on their side. They neither pique their curiosity, nor tempt their credulity, nor give them any chance to laugh at the cheat as a good joke. They are mere prosaic, common-place, and therefore unsuccessful, swindlers. Let them study Barnum's life; master the whole art and mystery of their business:—learn the advantage of doing things on a grand scale and with a flourish of trumpets:—steer clear of the embarrassments which jealous laws have thrown in the way of such pursuits:—and take courage from Barnum's success, as well as lessons from his experience. *Then* if they fail, the fault must be their own.

Nothing in this book is more remarkable than the obvious insensibility of Mr. Barnum to the real character of its disclosures. He takes an evident pride in the boldness and enormity of the impositions by which he has amassed his fortune. He does not confess them, he boasts of them. He has written his life for the sake of convincing the world—not that he is a moral or an up right man, not that he is capable of generous acts and of manly conduct—but that he is just the shrewdest and the sharpest Yankee that this hemisphere has yet produced. This is with him the highest point of ideal greatness. Whenever he chronicles an apparently noble and generous deed—such as his voluntary offer to make a more advantageous contract with Jenny Lind than the one she had accepted—he takes special pains to add that he did it on calculation, and from a selfish motive, and not from generosity or a sense of justice. He seems to fear that he shall be suspected of having sometimes acted without an eye to the main chance, and interpolates disclaimers into his narrative whenever they may seem to be required. There is an occasional intimation that this is done from an excess of candor, and to prevent the suspicion that he is claiming more credit than belongs to him; but this is intended only to make the impression more effective. Mr. Barnum is proud of his sagacity,—of his tact in playing upon the weaknesses of others, and of his skill in profiting by the public credulity. He feels that his strength lies in this faculty rather than in strict adherence to lofty morals and a nice sense of the rule of right. He accordingly sacrifices all other considerations to the desire of standing before the world as the most remarkable product of American genius in the art of making money. The whole book is written for this purpose, and all its incidents are skillfully adapted to produce the desired effect. He has shown very great invention in the variety of stories of his childhood and youth, his early experience and the various steps by which he ripened from very small beginnings, into the stupendous and magnificent master of the art of deception which he has since become. Judging from his book he seems to have been a humbug from his cradle. He would have it understood that he was born to the greatness he has since achieved. He cheated in long clothes, and had become an adept at practical jokes before he reached the dignity of a roundabout. In all this there is a good deal that is amusing, though, of course, no one is required, and probably not expected, to believe it. It is all part and parcel of the system which the book is written to reveal.

We confess our surprise that Mr. Barnum should have published this Autobiography, for we had given him credit for better judgment and more discretion. He had amassed a fortune, by means generally suspected to have not been scrupulously honorable, but which were very likely to be overlooked or forgotten in the more creditable and legitimate enterprises of his more recent life. His engagement of Jenny Lind was universally regarded as a public benefit, and evinced a bold sagacity which won him very great credit. He was establishing a reputation as a business man of marked ability, and was fast outliving the questionable reputation which public suspicion, rather than any known facts, had given him. He seems to have felt himself in same danger of subsiding into the common-place character of an enterprising, honest and successful man; so he has written this book to prevent the possibility of such a catastrophe. He has chosen his means with his usual sagacity; he will be quite as successful in this design, as in any of the others by which his life has been distinguished.

The book will be very widely read and will do infinite mischief. It will encourage the tendency, always too strong in the young men of this country, to seek fortune by other means than industry in the worthy pursuit of the honorable business on which the welfare of society depends. It will stimulate an eagerness for dashing experiments on public credulity, and multiply the numbers, already too large, of those who live by their wits, and seek fortune by pandering to the vices or the weaknesses of the public at large. We do not suppose it was Mr. Barnum's intention to exert such an influence when he wrote his life,—for its prevalent tone shows clearly his entire unconsciousness, that there is anything in his career which the noblest minded and the worthiest might not admire and emulate. But the book will have that effect, so far as it has any beyond the indulgence of that vapid curiosity which it has been the business of Mr. Barnum's life to stimulate and gratify.

THE CHRISTIAN REVIEW

Book Review of Life of P. T. Barnum

January 2, 1855

While many reviewers greeted Barnum's autobiography with horror, more than a few found it entertaining and generally harmless. Barnum's apologists often noted that whatever readers made of his exploits, it was hard to deny that he was a devout Christian and a powerful advocate of temperance, a cause that many evangelicals embraced at this time. This review, which appeared in a mainstream religious magazine of the era, took note of Barnum's other qualities, rendering a judgment in the showman's favor.

The Life of P. T. Barnum. Written by himself. (New York: Redfield. 1855. 12mo, pp. 404.) We are prepared to pronounce this one of the most amusing volumes we have ever read. . . . Mr. Barnum possesses a most exuberant love of fun. Indeed, he seems to have inherited the character of a joker from his maternal grandfather. The only improvement he has made upon the special proclivity of his ancestor, seems to be in the intensely practical turn which he has given to his jokes.

Undoubtedly many of the tricks which he has played upon the public, had their origin in this inherent propensity for gulling his friends. He certainly is not so oblivious of moral distinctions as he sometimes represents himself. We are glad to see that in this volume he has made a public acknowledgment of his profound reverence for the Bible as the word of God. We believe that he cherishes a sincere respect for sacred things. He is moreover, an earnest and efficient laborer in the cause of temperance. In this respect he has contributed much to the real prosperity of his fellows. By his merry-making disposition he provokes laughter, and so induces health. In so far he is a benefactor of his kind. When he shall become as devout as he is humane, he will prove a benefactor in a better sense and a far higher degree.

"Book Review of Life of P. T. Barnum," *The Christian Review,* January 2, 1855

3

View of the Exterior of Barnum's American Museum, New York City

1853

Barnum's American Museum, located at the present-day intersection of Broadway and Ann Street in New York City, was an illustration of Barnum's advice to aspiring entrepreneurs to "select the right location" when starting a business. This particular building occupied an extremely prominent place on the busiest thoroughfare of the largest city in the nation, drawing in crowds of passersby. But Barnum went further than most in drawing attention to his venue, plastering the walls and roofline with colorful posters that advertised the wonders of the museum; spotlights illuminated the building at night, making it the brightest place in a city of over a million people. The building burned down in 1867.

From The New York Public Library.

Iranistan, the Residence of Mr. Barnum
1851

In the late 1840s, Barnum hired the architect Leopold Eidlitz to design a new mansion just outside his adopted hometown of Bridgeport. The result was the ornate structure that Barnum dubbed Iranistan. Though nominally inspired by the Brighton Pavillion in England, the sixty-room structure drew upon myriad architectural traditions, creating something both recognizably exotic and entirely new. Barnum moved into the house in 1848 and often welcomed the public to its seventeen acres of fountains, gardens, and landscaped grounds. Left vacant after his bankruptcy in 1856, it burned down the following year.

IRANISTAN, THE RESIDENCE OF MR. BARNUM. *1851*

Courtesy Connecticut Historical Society.

P. T. Barnum and Tom Thumb

1850

Prior to Jenny Lind, Barnum's greatest success came with his promotion of the dwarf child Charles Stratton, whom he rechristened General Tom Thumb. Stratton quickly became an international sensation, one of the first modern celebrities, and an accomplished performer who entertained audiences with skits, antics, jokes, and other comic material that played off his small size. Here he appears with Barnum in a daguerreotype, a precursor to modern photographs.

National Portrait Gallery, Smithsonian Institution / Art Resource, NY.

6

WILLIAM SCHAUS

Panorama of Humbug

1850

After Barnum whipped Americans into a frenzy of excitement about the upcoming tour of Swedish opera singer Jenny Lind, critics sought to expose Barnum's manipulations. In this cartoon, a devil-like figure beats a drum to attract attention, while trumpets representing New York newspapers herald Lind's arrival. The barker calls out "Walk up Ladies & Gentlemen and see the greatest wonder of the age—the Real Swedish Nightingale, the only specimen in the Country." Barnum's American Museum looms in the background of the picture; Barnum himself lurks in the shadows, watching the spectacle from inside a doorway.

7

CURRIER & IVES

What Is It? Or, "Man Monkey"
circa 1860

Currier & Ives, a famous printer of colored engravings known as chromolithographs, produced a series of images of Barnum's "Gallery of Wonders" around the time of the Civil War. Here the "What Is It?" appears, surrounded by white museum patrons, in an image that sought to underscore the legitimacy of Barnum's "missing link." In reality, Barnum recruited a diminutive and deformed African American man to play the part, putting him in fur costumes and coaching him to perform a routine. This immensely popular—and deeply racist—entertainment remained a staple of Barnum's productions throughout the rest of his career. This exhibit appeared on the eve of the Civil War, when questions about race and slavery dominated politics and culture.

Currier & Ives / Museum of the City of New York 57.100.120.

An Heir to the Throne: Or the Next Republican Candidate

circa 1860

Barnum's "What Is It?" exhibit arrived at a moment when Abraham Lincoln, the nominee of the antislavery Republican Party, ran for the presidency. Proslavery Democrats, eager to stir up antagonism toward Lincoln, accused him of undermining white supremacy. Here, the figure of the "What Is It?" appears in the company of Horace Greeley, editor of the influential New York Tribune *newspaper and a power broker in the Republican Party, and Republican Abraham Lincoln, who would win the presidential election that year. Both men are shown hailing Barnum's creation as a future candidate for the Republican nomination.*

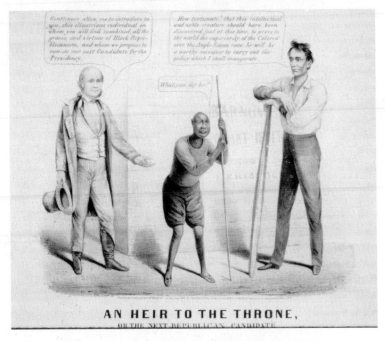

Library of Congress, Prints & Photographs Division, Reproduction number LCUSZC2-2564 (color film copy slide) LC-USZ6201997 (b&w film copy neg.).

What Is It?

circa 1860

The souvenir shop in Barnum's American Museum sold small photographs of some of the exhibits. This one memorializes the anonymous man who performed as "What Is It?" in the early 1860s. Unlike the other images that circulated, this one comes closer to capturing the real person who filled this role in Barnum's entertainment empire.

National Portrait Gallery, Smithsonian Institution / Art Resource, NY.

NEW YORK HERALD

Barnum and the Miniature Marriage

February 9, 1863

Barnum often stirred controversy by making money off matters that many critics believed should be kept separate from commerce. He hosted wildly successful "baby shows" that induced thousands of mothers to exhibit their infants in the hopes of winning cash prizes. In 1863, he staged the public wedding of Tom Thumb and another of his dwarf performers, Lavinia Warren. The event was wildly successful—and controversial, as this assessment makes clear.

BARNUM AND THE MINIATURE MARRIAGE

The American press and public have been exceedingly lenient with Barnum. They have allowed him to make money by humbagging innocent people, and more money by selling a book telling how well his humbugs have succeeded. Recently, however, he has taken altogether too bold an advantage of this leniency. Having secured a dwarf woman, he has been exhibiting her at his Museum for some time past as the betrothed of another dwarf called General Tom Thumb. How this match was arranged we do not care to know; but we are informed that it is to be consummated at Grace church to-morrow with all the display of a fashionable wedding. Of course we have no objections to the marriage, and no desire to forbid the banns. Miss Warren is a woman and Tom Thumb is a man, no matter how small they may be, and they have as good a right to be wedded as any other man and woman. This will be by no means the first time that dwarfs have been married and lived happily-ever after. We do object, however, to Barnum's share in the transaction, and particularly to his attempt to make money by the public exhibition of the intended bride and all the paraphernalia of the affair.

"Barnum and the Miniature Marriage," *New York Herald*, February 9, 1863.

By his connection with this miniature marriage, Barnum has injured himself sadly in the estimation of virtuous people. There is such a thing as going a little too far even with patrons so indulgent as the Americans. The marriage vows ought not to be trified with for the interest of a showman. The exhibition of Miss Warren at the Museum, the display of Miss Warren's wedding dress, Tom Thumb's wedding shirt, Miss Warren's wedding shoes and Tom Thumb's wedding stockings in store windows on Broadway, and all the other details of Barnum's management of this matter, are offensive to delicacy, decorum, modesty and good taste.

11

MATTHEW BRADY

Tom Thumb and Lavinia Warren

circa 1863

Matthew Brady is best known today for his searing photographs of Civil War battlefields. But his studio, located across the street from Barnum's American Museum, also took thousands of photographs of the human curiosities whom Barnum promoted. This staged image, which claimed to show the wedding of Tom Thumb and Lavinia Warren, was shot the same year as the Battle of Gettysburg. When the couple made their way to Washington, D.C., after the ceremony, President Lincoln interrupted a cabinet meeting to wish them well.

Photograph by Mathew Brady/Granger, NYC.

12

P. T. BARNUM

Humbugs of the World: An Account of Humbugs, Delusions, Impositions, Quackeries, Deceits, and Deceivers Generally, in All Ages

1866

In 1866, Barnum published an exposé of various frauds, cheats, and impostures of the age: sham investments, patent medicines, bogus paranormal activity, swindlers, and other attempts to prey on the naïve and credulous. In this book and elsewhere, Barnum took pains to distinguish his own entertainments from these other impositions. In the introduction to the volume—reprinted here—the showman offers his own, idiosyncratic definition of "humbug."

... The greatest humbug of all is the man who believes—or pretends to believe—that everything and everybody are humbugs. We sometimes meet a person who professes that there is no virtue; that every man has his price, and every woman hers; that any statement from anybody is just as likely to be false as true, and that the only way to decide which, is to consider whether truth or a lie was likely to have paid best in that particular case. Religion he thinks one of the smartest business dodges extant, a firstrate investment, and by all odds the most respectable disguise that a lying or swindling business man can wear. Honor he thinks is a sham. Honesty he considers a plausible word to flourish in the eyes of the greener portion of our race, as you would hold out a cabbage leaf to coax a donkey. What people want, he thinks, or says he thinks, is something good to eat, something good to drink, fine clothes, luxury, laziness, wealth. If you can imagine a hog's mind in a man's body—sensual, greedy, selfish, cruel, cunning, sly, coarse, yet stupid, short-sighted, unreasoning, unable to comprehend anything except what concerns the flesh, you have your man. He thinks himself

P. T. Barnum, Humbugs of the World: An Account of Humbugs, Delusions, Impositions, Quackeries, Deceits, and Deceivers Generally, in All Ages (New York: Carleton, 1866), 16–21.

philosophic and practical, a man of the world; he thinks to show knowledge and wisdom, penetration, deep acquaintance with men and things. Poor fellow! he has exposed his own nakedness. Instead of showing that others are rotten inside, he has proved that he is. He claims that it is not safe to believe others—it is perfectly safe to disbelieve him. He claims that every man will get the better of you if possible—let him alone! Selfishness, he says, is the universal rule—leave nothing to depend on his generosity or honor; trust him just as far as you can sling an elephant by the tail. A bad world, he sneers, full of deceit and nastiness—it is his own foul breath that he smells; only a thoroughly corrupt heart could suggest such vile thoughts. He sees only what suits him, as a turkey-buzzard spies only carrion, though amid the loveliest landscape. I pronounce him who thus virtually slanders his father and dishonors his mother and defiles the sanctities of home and the glory of patriotism and the merchant's honor and the martyr's grave and the saint's crown—who does not even know that every sham shows that there is a reality, and that hypocrisy is the homage that vice pays to virtue—I pronounce him—no, I do not pronounce him a humbug, the word does not apply to him. He is a fool.

Looked at on one side, the history of humbug is truly humiliating to intellectual pride, yet the long silly story is less absurd during the later ages of history, and grows less and less so in proportion to the spread of real Christianity. This religion promotes good sense, actual knowledge, contentment with what we cannot help, and the exclusive use of intelligent means for increasing human happiness and decreasing human sorrow. And whenever the time shall come when men are kind and just and honest; when they only want what is fair and right, judge only on real and true evidence, and take nothing for granted, then there will be no place left for any humbugs, either harmless or hurtful.

Upon a careful consideration of my undertaking to give an account of the "Humbugs of the World," I find myself somewhat puzzled in regard to the true definition of that word. To be sure, Webster says that humbug, as a noun, is an "imposition under fair pretences;" and as a verb, it is "to deceive; to impose on." With all due deference to Doctor Webster, I submit that, according to present usage, this is not the only, nor even the generally accepted definition of that term.

We will suppose, for instance, that a man with "fair pretences" applies to a wholesale merchant for credit on a large bill of goods. His "fair pretences" comprehend an assertion that he is a moral and religious man, a member of the church, a man of wealth, etc., etc. It turns out that he is not worth a dollar, but is a base, lying wretch, an impostor and a cheat. He is arrested and imprisoned for "obtaining property under false pretences" or, as Webster says, "fair pretences." He is punished for his villainy. The public do not call him a "humbug;" they very properly term him a swindler.

A man, bearing the appearance of a gentleman in dress and manners, purchases property from you, and with "fair pretences" obtains your confidence. You find, when he has left, that he paid you with counterfeit bank-notes, or a forged draft. This man is justly called a "forger," or "counterfeiter;" and if arrested, he is punished as such; but nobody thinks of calling him a "humbug."

A respectable-looking man sits by your side in an omnibus or rail-car. He converses fluently, and is evidently a man of intelligence and reading. He attracts your attention by his "fair pretences." Arriving at your journey's end, you miss your watch and your pocket-book. Your fellow passenger proves to be the thief. Everybody calls him a "pickpocket," and not withstanding his "fair pretences," not a person in the community calls him a "humbug."

Two actors appear as stars at two rival theatres. They are equally talented, equally pleasing. One advertises himself simply as a tragedian, under his proper name—the other boasts that he is a prince, and wears decorations presented by all the potentates of the world, including the "King of the Cannibal Islands." He is correctly set down as a "humbug," while this term is never applied to the other actor. But if the man who boasts of having received a foreign title is a miserable actor, and he gets up gift-enterprises and bogus entertainments, or pretends to devote the proceeds of his tragic efforts to some charitable object, without, in fact, doing so—he is then a humbug in Dr. Webster's sense of that word, for he is an "impostor under fair pretences."

Two physicians reside in one of our fashionable avenues. They were both educated in the best medical colleges; each has passed an examination, received his diploma, and been dubbed an M. D. They are equally skilled in the healing art. One rides quietly about the city in his gig or brougham, visiting his patients without noise or clamor—the other sallies out in his coach and four, preceded by a band of music, and his carriage and horses are covered with handbills and placards, announcing his "wonderful cures." This man is properly called a quack and a humbug. Why? Not because he cheats or imposes upon the public, for he does not, but because, as generally understood, "humbug" consists in putting on glittering appearances—outside show—novel expedients, by which to suddenly arrest public attention, and attract the public eye and ear.

Clergymen, lawyers, or physicians, who should resort to such methods of attracting the public, would not, for obvious reasons, be apt to succeed. Bankers, insurance-agents, and others, who aspire to become the custodians of the money of their fellow-men, would require a different species of advertising from this; but there are various trades and occupations which need only notoriety to insure success, always provided that when customers are once attracted, they never fail to get their money's worth. An honest man who thus arrests public attention will be called a "humbug," but he is not a swindler or an impostor. If, however, after attracting crowds of customers by his unique displays, a man foolishly fails to give them a full equivalent for their money, they never patronize him a second time, but they very properly denounce him as a swindler, a cheat, an impostor; they do not, however, call him a "humbug." He fails, not because he advertises his wares in an *outre* manner, but because, after attracting crowds of patrons, he stupidly and wickedly cheats them. . . .

13

HARPER'S WEEKLY

A Colossal Enterprise

March 27, 1875

After the second American Museum burned down in 1868, Barnum launched a series of massive traveling shows that combined many of his classic exhibits with a new menagerie of exotic animals, jugglers, clowns, acrobats, and other performers. This article, from Harper's Weekly, *captures the scale and substance of Barnum's Gilded Age entertainments. By the 1880s, Barnum claimed to have the "Greatest Show on Earth," which traveled around the country and the world.*

Ten years ago there was still standing on the corner of Broadway and Ann Street, where the stately Herald building now overlooks the busiest thoroughfare in the New World, a large, rambling structure, of

"A Colossal Enterprise," *Harper's Weekly,* March 27, 1875.

rather shabby external appearance, which was known to all the world of America as a veritable Palace of Wonders. Pictures of the strange animals from every part of the globe, which were to be seen within, adorned the outer walls, and stimulated the curiosity of the passers-by; the flags of all nations waved from the parapets, and above them proudly floated the Stars and Stripes. From sunrise till late at night throngs of people, of all ages, passed in at its ample doors and wandered through its halls, lingering at every step to wonder and admire. A larger or more wonderful collection of curiosities was never gathered under a single roof; and though many of them were of little intrinsic value, a very large proportion would have been of great worth to any museum. There was something to catch every variety of taste. For the lovers of the marvelous there were monstrosities like the "woolly horse," the "What is it?" and the "Mermaid;" for those who took delight in natural history there was the sea-lion, the learned seal, the Happy Family, the stuffed walrus, and many another interesting specimen of the animal kingdom from the Rocky Mountains, the burning wilds of Africa, the icy regions of the arctic zone, or from the uttermost isles of the ocean. In short, the whole world was laid under tribute to furnish entertainment to the patrons of the American Museum. The sea gave its strangest forms of fish and shell, the forest and the desert their savage denizens, the air its varied shapes of feathered beauty. Relics of Indian times, of our colonial days, and of our great War of Independence attracted those who were interested in American antiquities; suits of battered armor, dinted shields, battle-axes of uncouth and frightful shape, spears, swords, daggers, and other ancient weapons, carried the visitor back to the days when men fought hand to hand, instead of picking each other off, like game, with rifles, or sweeping whole regiments down with the deadly mitrailleuse [a forerunner of the modern machine gun].

Then there was the lecture-room, or theatre, where Sothern, Barney Williams, and other well-known actors won their first laurels, before audiences that could not often afford to treat themselves to an evening's amusement at the more expensive theatres. The transient attractions of the Museum were constantly varied. There were "living statuary," pantomime, instrumental music, ventriloquism, Punch and Judy, fancy glass-blowing, jugglery, etc., and when this marvelous building, with all its contents, was destroyed by fire, on the 13th of July, 1865, the community sustained a loss that neither time nor money could retrieve. Mr. Barnum, it is true, soon established a new museum higher up on Broadway, where he gathered an admirable collection of curiosities, but it did not compare with the old. "The second Temple was not like the first."

These reminiscences of the old American Museum, which is still held in affectionate remembrance by a large portion of the community, are naturally suggested by the announcement of Mr. Barnum's latest and most gigantic enterprise, the "Great Roman Hippodrome," with which he proposes to travel through the States during the coming season. His preparations are on a scale of magnificence unrivaled in the history of traveling exhibitions. All his shows have been merged in a chartered corporation, known as "The P. T. Barnum Universal Exposition Company," with a capital of a million of dollars. Mr. Barnum, who is president of the company, and his manager, Mr. Coup, have spent months in Europe, visiting every important exhibition, and bringing away many choice features and valuable suggestions, and the result is a combination of attractions, such as has never been seen in one exhibition since the world began.

The Great Roman Hippodrome will resemble a moving camp. There are 1200 men, women, and children in Mr. Barnum's service, and the stock includes 750 horses and ponies, besides elephants, camels, English stags and stag-hounds, trained ostriches, lions, bears, tigers, and other animals. For the exhibition of the menagerie and the various shows, displays, and performances connected with the enterprise, two enormous tents, each 500 feet in length and 300 in width, have been provided, one of which will be kept in advance, in order that no time may be lost by delay in making ready. The question of transportation by rail—a very serious one—was solved by the construction of 150 cars, twice the usual length, built expressly for this purpose. Among them are a number of "horse-palace" cars, constructed with commodious stalls, in which the horses can lie down and rest while on the journey, and arrive at the place of exhibition quite fresh for the performance. Besides moving the tents, animals, and all other material in these Hippodrome cars, berths will be provided in those devoted to the personnel of the company for nearly all the employees. Besides the great exhibition tents, there are cooking and dining tents, and stable tents for the horses and other animals. There is also attached to the company a large corps of blacksmiths and carpenters and builders, some of whom precede the show several days, to make ready for the exhibition by preparing the ground, erecting seats, etc. The dressing-room tents alone will cover more ground than an ordinary circus.

To move such an enormous establishment without hitch or delay requires the employment of clear-headed, practical men at the head of each department. Every thing is so arranged as to move with the smoothness and precision of clock-work. At the appointed hour the canvas will go up, the street procession will move, the performances will commence. When all is over, and the great tent emptied, every thing will be packed up by those detailed for the work, and the caravan, without the loss of a minute, will be on the move toward the next place of exhibition.

The programme of performances will be varied and attractive. Donaldson will make daily balloon ascensions with a car large enough to contain a company of five or six persons, at a cost of about $500 a day for this feature alone. Then there will be the "Roman races" in chariots driven by "Amazons," the "liberty races," in which forty wild horses are turned loose in the arena in exact imitation of the famous carnival races of Rome and Naples; the "standing races," in which the riders stand on bare-back horses; hurdle races for ladies; flat races by English, French, and American jockeys; besides camel, elephant, ostrich, and monkey races. Another feature will be exhibitions of Indian life on the plains, in which the actors will be scores of Indians, with their squaws and pappooses. They will put up a genuine Indian encampment, hunt real buffaloes, give war-dances, pony races, foot races against horses, exhibitions of daring horsemanship, lasso-throwing. A band of Mexican raiders, mounted on their famous mustangs, will make a pretended attack on the Indian camp, and give a mimic but faithful representation of the wild scenes enacted on the Western frontier. The English stag-hunt will be an exact picture of the sport itself, with a company of 150 men and women in full hunting costume, and a large pack of English stag hounds. There will also be many other interesting and attractive features, the mere mention of which would make a small volume.

Mr. Barnum certainly deserves great credit for an enterprise which is calculated to afford a vast amount of innocent, popular amusement; and although this gigantic venture involves an enormous outlay of money, it will present too many attractions not to be generously sustained. It is Mr. Barnum's intention to visit Europe next autumn with the whole establishment, and astonish the Old World with this wonderful exposition of what can be accomplished by Yankee enterprise.

14

NEW YORK TIMES

Obituary of P. T. Barnum

April 8, 1891

When Barnum died on April 7, 1891, eulogists sought to capture the full sweep of his career. This essay, which appeared in the same paper that once condemned his autobiography, offered one of the more philosophical meditations on the meaning of Barnum's long and colorful life.

There is hardly an American now in the vigor of life who can remember when the name of Barnum was not familiar to him, and there are very few Americans who do not feel that they owe him a certain debt of gratitude for brightening their lives or the lives of their children. It is really wonderful and unexampled, the career that closed yesterday. Since the beginnings of history there has been no showman to be compared to the showman whose long connection with the show business is now broken. To a great many people the first thought that his death brings is that he was the prince of humbugs, but this is a notion altogether false and inadequate. It was his pride and boast, from the beginning of his career until the end of it, that he gave the people who went to see his various and diverse shows "the worth of their money." The boast was justified, and so was the pride. "The rude man," according to Goethe, "is satisfied to see something going on," and it was to the rude man, the average man—the grown-up child, in a word—as well as to the actual child, that Barnum undertook to cater. His success in hitting the taste of the child, adolescent or adult, was the success of his enterprises, and it was quite wonderful with what tact and nicety he managed to hit this taste. No child of ripe or unripe years ever left his show, whatever it might have been, without the consciousness of having been amused to the value of the charge for admission. To real children he was a great benefactor, and how many generations of children has he benefited!

It cannot be denied that there was a flavor of humbug about many of Barnum's announcements, especially in his early and struggling years. Those who remember "Joyce Heth," the Woolly Horse, the Mermaid, and

---

"Obituary of P. T. Barnum," *New York Times*, April 8, 1891, p. 4.

144

the "What Is It" will agree that, in respect of these things, the show did not entirely come up to the bills, and that there were elements of doubt about these curiosities. Indeed, Barnum himself confessed the unreality of some of these attractions in his autobiographies with a frankness that leaves nothing to be desired and that quite disarms criticism. After an attraction had served his turn, he had no further interest in maintaining its genuineness. But it would be a great mistake to assume on this account that his show was ever mostly or largely composed of objects that were other than they were represented to be. The child in years or the child in intellectual development was never heard to complain that he had been deceived. Even if he had been lured into the show for the sake of seeing something that was not altogether what his artful tempter had represented it to be, he always found enough to repay his curiosity.

It may seem odd, but we believe it to be true, that what distinguished Barnum from other public entertainers of equal or nearly equal conspicuousness was really the absence of humbug. Poetical statements about particular objects are by no means so mischievous, either to him who makes them or to him who accepts them, as a deceptive statement about the character of an entertainment in general, with which so many showmen deceive their patrons and themselves. Barnum was never under any illusions, nor did he ever encourage any illusions, about the nature of his function. He did not pretend to be an evangelist or an artist, but simply a showman. He might not have been willing to make oath to all his advertisements, but he never disguised the fact that he was in "the show business," and that he meant to give the public what it wanted. If in any instance he failed, he did not blame the public for its failure to appreciate the moral or æsthetic lesson he had endeavored to inculcate. He simply dropped the unsuccessful feature, and substituted something else that was likely to prove more attractive. This is not, perhaps, a very lofty vocation, and it has no pretense of being a "mission," but there is nothing dishonest or offensive about it. It is only when a man who is in fact a showman pretends to be an evangelist or an artist, and blames his public for his failure to entertain it, that he becomes a real and thorough humbug. There are specimens enough and to spare in the world of this kind of showman, but Barnum was not one of them. Whether he was managing Jenny Lind or Tom Thumb or a circus, he did not pretend to be anything but a showman or that his entertainment was anything but a show. The "rude man" could never justly have objected to it that he failed to find "something going on." As a show it was always lively and acceptable, and the man who presented it will always be remembered with kindness by the successive generations of children whom, in its various phases, it has entertained.

A Barnum Chronology (1810–1891)

1810 Phineas Taylor Barnum born July 5 in Bethel, Connecticut.

1825 Barnum's father, Philo Barum, dies after long illness on September 7.

1827 Moves to Brooklyn, New York, to clerk in a store owned by a relative, Oliver Taylor.

1828 Moves back to Bethel and opens a small grocery store; begins selling lottery tickets.

1829 Marries Charity Hallett of Danbury, Connecticut, on November 8.

1831 Opens new, larger country store in Bethel with an uncle in July.

Begins publishing newspaper in Bethel called the *Herald of Freedom* on October 19.

1832 Sued for libel by rival grocery keeper in Bethel; spends sixty days in Danbury jail.

1833 First child, Caroline Cordelia Barnum, born May 27.

1834 Leaves editorship of the *Herald of Freedom*; moves family to New York City.

1835 Leases the slave Joice Heth on August 6; begins exhibiting her around the country.

1836 Joice Heth dies on February 19; Barnum stages public dissection the following week.

Takes traveling circus on the road, traveling throughout the country until May 1837.

1837 Forms new traveling circus and tours until June 1838.

1838 Forms partnership in New York City to make paste, bear's grease [a topical ointment that was rumored to cure baldness], and cologne water.

1840 Dissolves partnership after business partner swindles him; resumes touring circus.

Second child, Helen Maria Barnum, born April 18.

1841 Purchases Scudder's American Museum, a collection of curiosities, for $14,000.

1842 Purchases and begins exhibiting the "Feejee Mermaid" at the American Museum.

Third child, Frances Irena Barnum, born May 1; dies in 1844.

Hires Charles Stratton, the child dwarf, renaming him "General Tom Thumb."

Purchases Peale's American Museum, adding to the collections of the American Museum.

1844 Leaves for tour of Europe with Tom Thumb; returns in April 1846, though Barnum made two visits to the United States during this time.

1846 Fourth child, Pauline Taylor Barnum, born March 1.

1848 Moves into Iranistan, an ornate mansion built outside of Bridgeport, Connecticut.

1850 Signs Swedish opera star Jenny Lind; she arrives in New York on September 1.

1851 Launches "Barnum's Great Asiatic Caravan, Museum, and Menagerie" on May 5.

Barnum's management of Lind concludes June 9.

Launches commercial development of East Bridgeport.

1854 Publishes the first edition of the Autobiography in December.

1855 Makes fateful investment in the Jerome Manufacturing Company.

1856 Goes bankrupt and spends most of the year negotiating with his creditors.

1857 Visits England with Tom Thumb; Iranistan burns down in December.

1858 Returns to England and first gives "Art of Money Getting" speech on December 29.

1860 Regains control of the American Museum on March 24.

1862 Assumes management of "Commodore Nutt," another dwarf.

1863 Sponsors wedding of Tom Thumb and Lavinia Warren in New York City.

1865 Elected to the Connecticut General Assembly in April.

The American Museum burns down; Barnum reopens at a new location.

1867 Runs for the U.S. House of Representatives but is defeated.

1868 The second American Museum burns down in March.

1870 Launches "Barnum's Grand Traveling Museum, Menagerie, Caravan, and Circus."

1873 Charity Barnum dies after a long illness on November 19.

1874 Launches the "Great Roman Hippodrome," an even larger traveling circus, in April.

Marries Nancy Fish, a British woman 40 years his junior.

1875 Elected mayor of Bridgeport, Connecticut.

1881 Partners with circus promoter James A. Bailey.

1882 Introduces "Jumbo," an enormous African elephant, to American audiences.

1883 Endows the Barnum Museum of Natural History at Tufts University.

1891 Dies April 7; buried in Mountain Grove Cemetery, Bridgeport, Connecticut.

Questions for Consideration

1. How did the pranks of Barnum's childhood shape his entertainments?
2. Why was Barnum drawn to high-risk business enterprises?
3. Why did reviewers of Barnum's memoirs object to its publication?
4. How did Barnum involve his audiences in his many exhibits?
5. How did Barnum create interest in his attractions before they opened?
6. Why does Barnum rarely mention his family life in the memoirs?
7. What role did advertising play in Barnum's business success?
8. How did Barnum's views on race and slavery evolve over his life? Why?
9. Did Barnum exploit his sideshow curiosities, or did they participate, too?
10. How did cities, and New York City in particular, define Barnum?
11. Why did customers pay money to see exhibits they suspected were fake?
12. How did Barnum's promotion of Joice Heth differ from that of Jenny Lind?
13. What role did debt play in Barnum's successes and failures?
14. How do modern museums compare with Barnum's American Museum?
15. How do Barnum's business tactics remain relevant today? Give examples.
16. How did the sectional crisis and the Civil War change Barnum?
17. What does Barnum's career tell us about capitalism in his lifetime?

Selected Bibliography

The version of the *Life of P. T. Barnum* reproduced here is an abridged version of the first edition published by Redfield in 1854. Barnum revised and sanitized his memoirs in six additional editions, possibly more. But aside from the original 1854 edition, the two most important later versions are *Struggles and Triumphs; Or, Forty Years' Recollections of P. T. Barnum* (Buffalo: Warren Johnson, 1872), and the final edition published shortly before his death: *Struggles and Triumphs; Or, Sixty Years' Recollections of P. T. Barnum* (Buffalo: Courier Company, 1889).

Barnum was a prolific writer. Aside from his widely read exposé of fraud, *The Humbugs of the World* (New York, Carleton, 1866), he authored numerous newspaper articles and pamphlets on diverse subjects. He also wrote a fictionalized autobiography called *Adventures of an Adventurer*, which appeared in serialized form in the *New York Atlas* in 1841. Many of these writings have been painstakingly compiled and edited by historian James Cook in *The Colossal P. T. Barnum Reader* (Urbana and Chicago: University of Illinois Press, 2005). Some of Barnum's private letters have also been edited and published; see, for example, A. H. Saxon, ed., *Selected Letters of P. T. Barnum* (New York: Columbia University Press, 1983).

Barnum has attracted the attention of many biographers. The best, perhaps, is A. H. Saxon's *P. T. Barnum: The Legend and the Man* (New York: Columbia University Press, 1989), though two others merit a mention: Irving Wallace, *The Fabulous Showman: The Life and Times of P. T. Barnum* (New York: Knopf, 1959), and Philip B. Kunhardt Jr., Philip B. Kunhardt III, and Peter W. Kunhardt, *P. T. Barnum: America's Greatest Showman* (New York: Knopf, 1995). The latter, written to accompany a television documentary on Barnum, is copiously illustrated.

A number of scholars have written insightful accounts of how Barnum fits into the larger history of American popular culture. The earliest was Constance Rourke, *Trumpets of Jubilee* (New York: Harcourt Brace, 1927), which treats Barnum as well as several other cultural figures of the era. More recent and comprehensive works include Neil Harris,

Humbug: The Art of P. T. Barnum (Chicago: University of Chicago, 1975), and Bluford Adams, *E Pluribus Barnum: The Great Showman and the Making of U.S. Popular Culture* (Minneapolis: University of Minnesota Press, 1997). On Barnum and the larger culture of fraud, see James W. Cook, *The Arts of Deception: Playing with Fraud in the Age of Barnum* (Cambridge, MA: Harvard University Press, 2001), and Edward J. Balleisen, *Fraud: An American History from Barnum to Madoff* (Princeton, NJ: Princeton University Press, 2017).

In addition, several historians have examined particular episodes in Barnum's career as well as the people he promoted. On Joice Heth, see Benjamin Reiss, *The Showman and the Slave: Race, Death, and Memory in Barnum's America* (Cambridge, MA: Harvard University Press, 2001). On Tom Thumb, see Raymund Fitzsimons, *Barnum in London* (New York: St. Martin's Press, 1970) and Eric D. Lehman, *Becoming Tom Thumb: Charles Stratton, P. T. Barnum, and the Dawn of American Celebrity* (Middletown, CT: Wesleyan University Press, 2013). On Barnum's promotion of Jenny Lind, see W. Porter Ware and Thaddeus C. Lockard Jr., *P. T. Barnum Presents Jenny Lind: The American Tour of the Swedish Nightingale* (Baton Rouge: Louisiana State University Press, 1980). For more on the famous "Siamese Twins" Chang and Eng, see Joseph Andrew Orser, *The Lives of Chang and Eng: Siam's Twins in Nineteenth-Century America* (Chapel Hill: University of North Carolina Press, 2014).

Students interested in learning more about the genres of entertainment that Barnum helped pioneer or promote can turn to several related works. On blackface minstrelsy, see Robert Toll, *Blacking Up: The Minstrel Show in Nineteenth-Century America* (New York: Oxford University Press, 1974); William J. Mahar, *Behind the Burnt Cork Mask: Early Blackface Minstrelsy and Antebellum American Culture* (Urbana and Chicago: University of Illinois Press, 1998); and Eric Lott, *Love and Theft: Blackface Minstrelsy and the American Working Class* (New York: Oxford University Press, 1993).

For more on the American Museum, its antecedents, and its competitors, see Charles Coleman Sellers, *Mr. Peale's Museum: Charles Wilson Peale and the First Popular Museum of Natural Science and Art* (Philadelphia: Barra Foundation, 1980); William T. Alderson, ed., *Mermaids, Mummies, and Mastodons: The Emergence of the American Museum* (Washington, D.C.: The American Association of Museums, 1991); David Rodney Brigham, *Public Culture in the Early Republic: Peale's Museum and Its Audience* (Washington, D.C.: Smithsonian Institution

Press, 1995); and Andrea Stulman Dennett, *Weird and Wonderful: The Dime Museum in America* (New York: NYU Press, 1997).

On sideshow freaks, with some focused discussion of Barnum's exhibits, see Robert Bogdan, *Freak Show: Presenting Human Oddities for Amusement and Profit* (Chicago: University of Chicago Press, 1988), and Rosemarie Garland Thomson, ed., *Freakery: Cultural Spectacles of the Extraordinary Body* (New York: NYU Press, 1996). A less academic take on the subject can be found in Mark Hartzman, *American Sideshow: An Encyclopedia of History's Most Wondrous and Curiously Strange Performers* (New York: Penguin, 2005).

Several works cover the different kinds of traveling shows and circuses that Barnum promoted throughout his career. See, for example, Robert Lewis, ed., *From Traveling Show to Vaudeville: Theatrical Spectacle in America, 1830–1910* (Baltimore: Johns Hopkins University Press, 2007), and Janet Davis, *The Circus Age: Culture and Society under the American Big Top* (Chapel Hill: University of North Carolina Press, 2002). The history of the circus in New York City is the focus of Matthew Wittman, *The Circus and the City: New York, 1793–2010* (New York: Bard Graduate Center for the Decorative Arts, 2012).

While the Internet has many sources on Barnum, one of the more serious, sustained examinations of his career, focusing in particular on the American Museum, can be found at http://lostmuseum.cuny.edu/. It contains a useful introduction to Barnum's career as well as additional essays and documents on Barnum's most famous emporium of entertainment.

Index